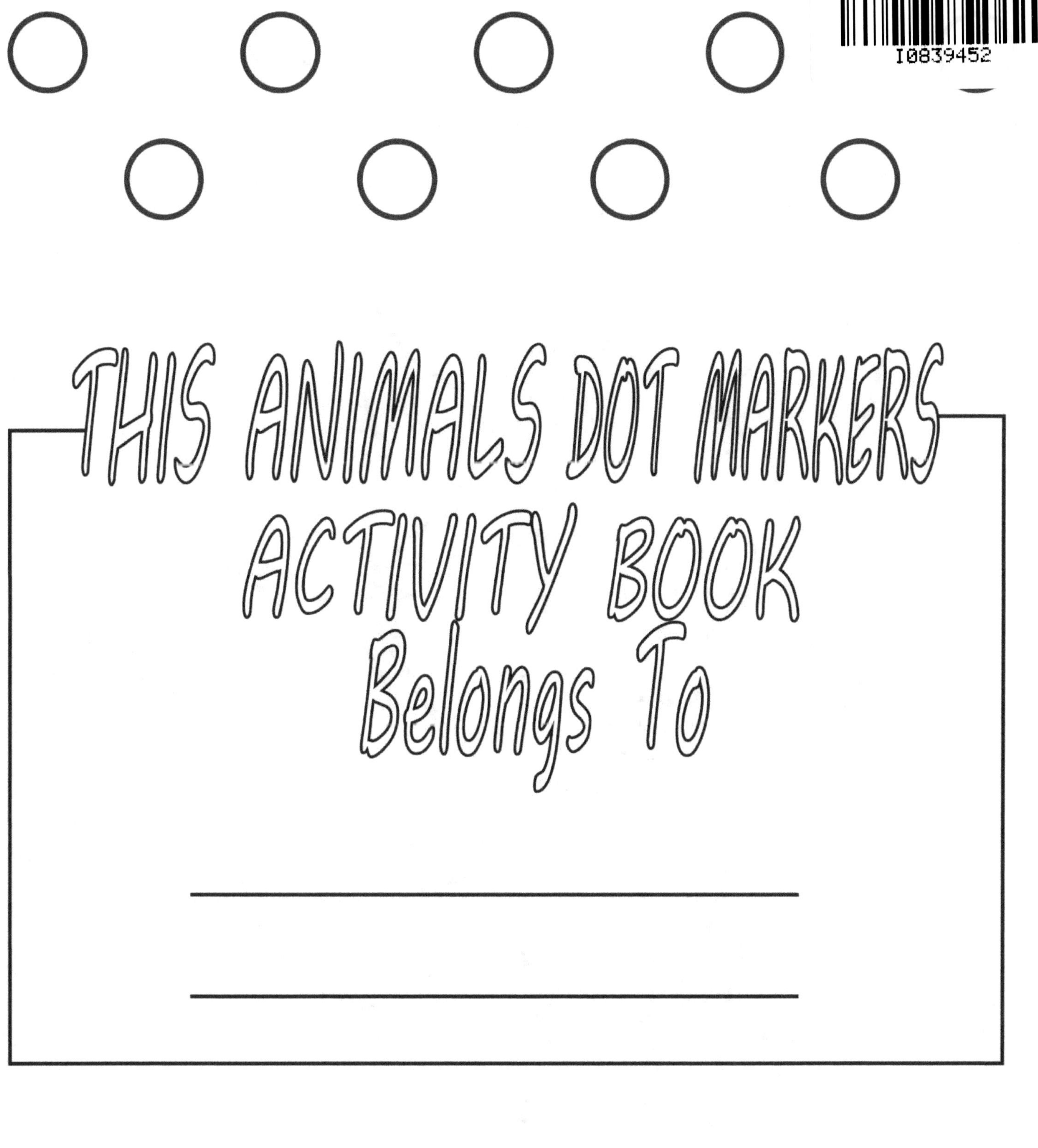

THIS ANIMALS DOT MARKERS
ACTIVITY BOOK
Belongs To

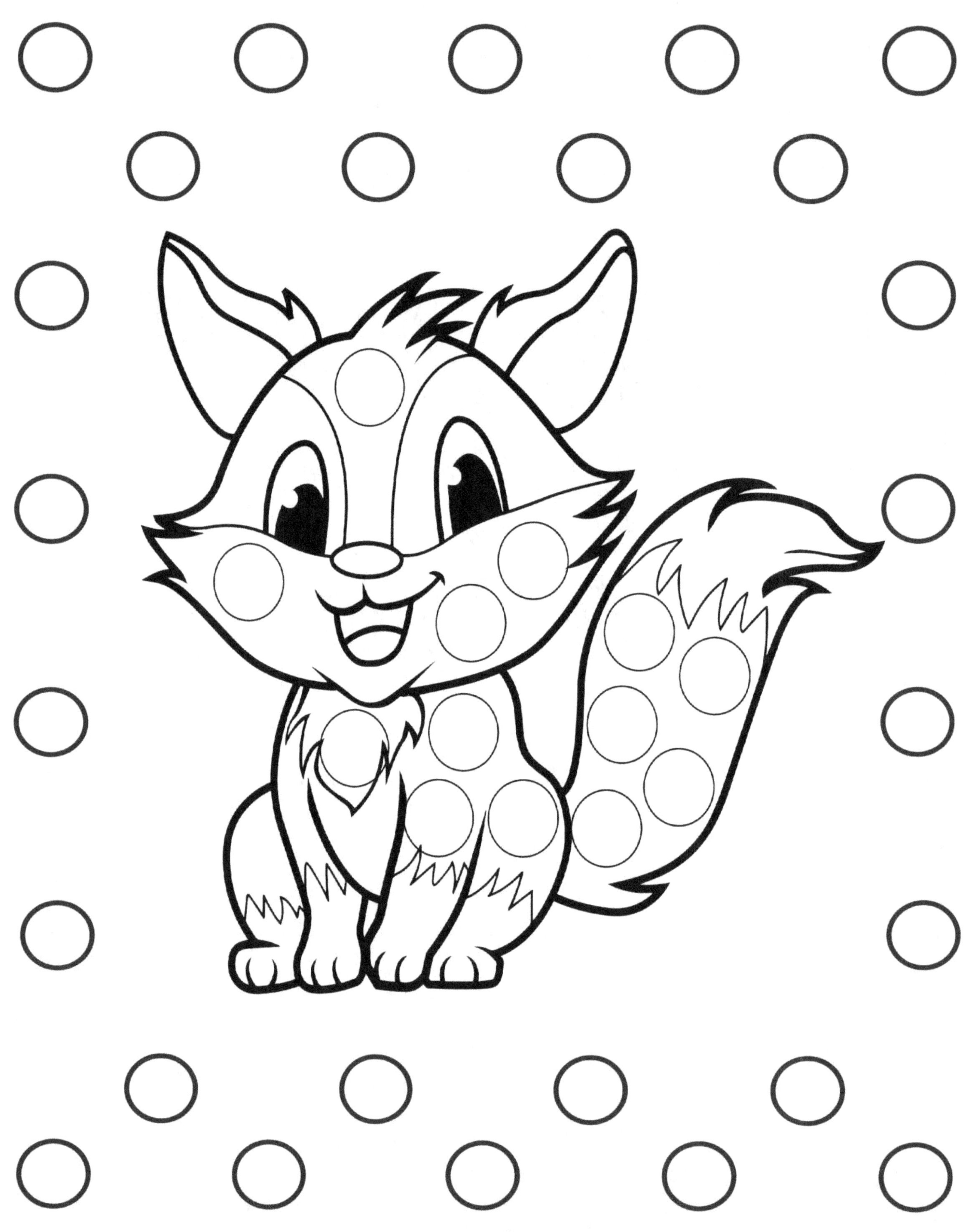

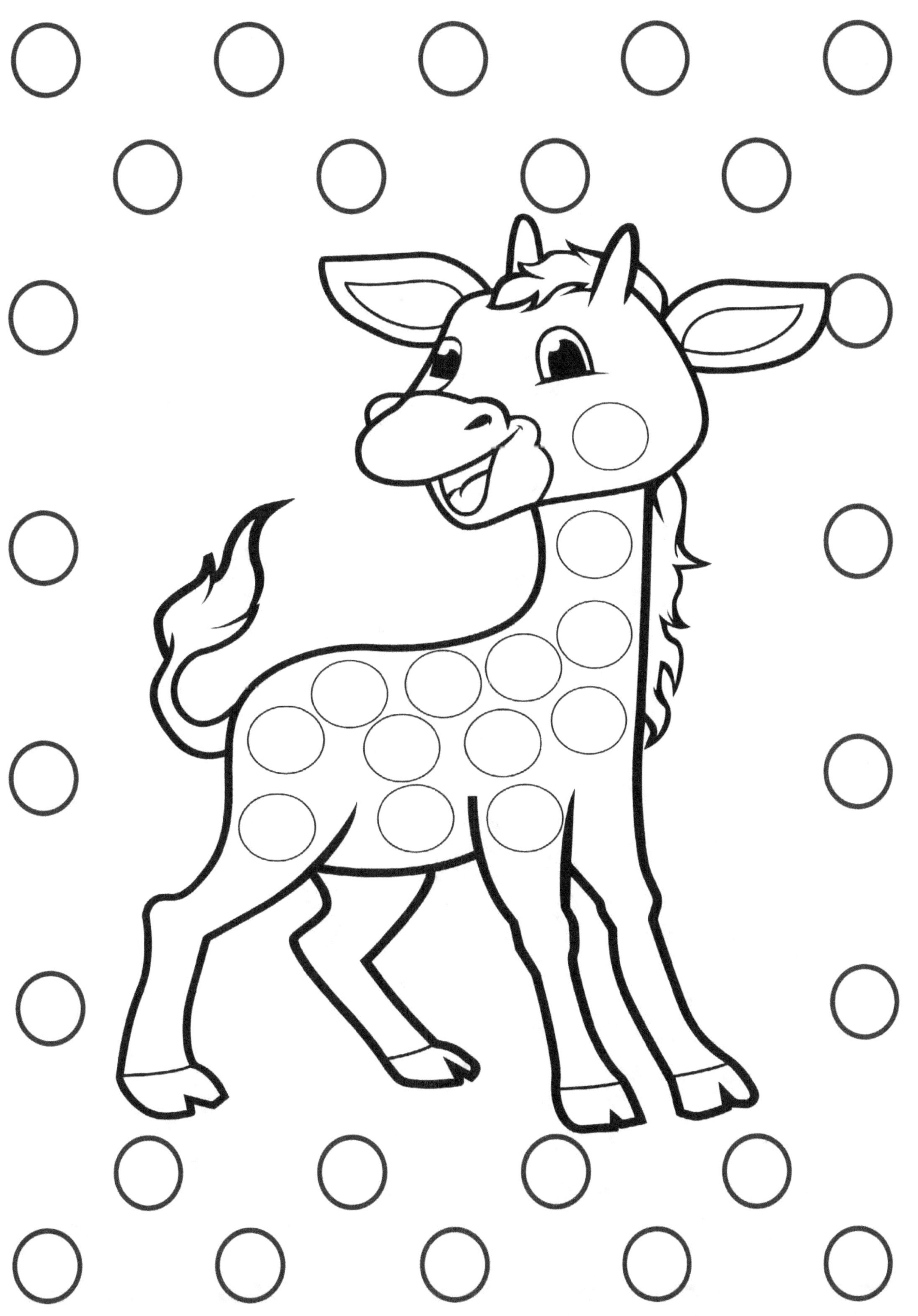

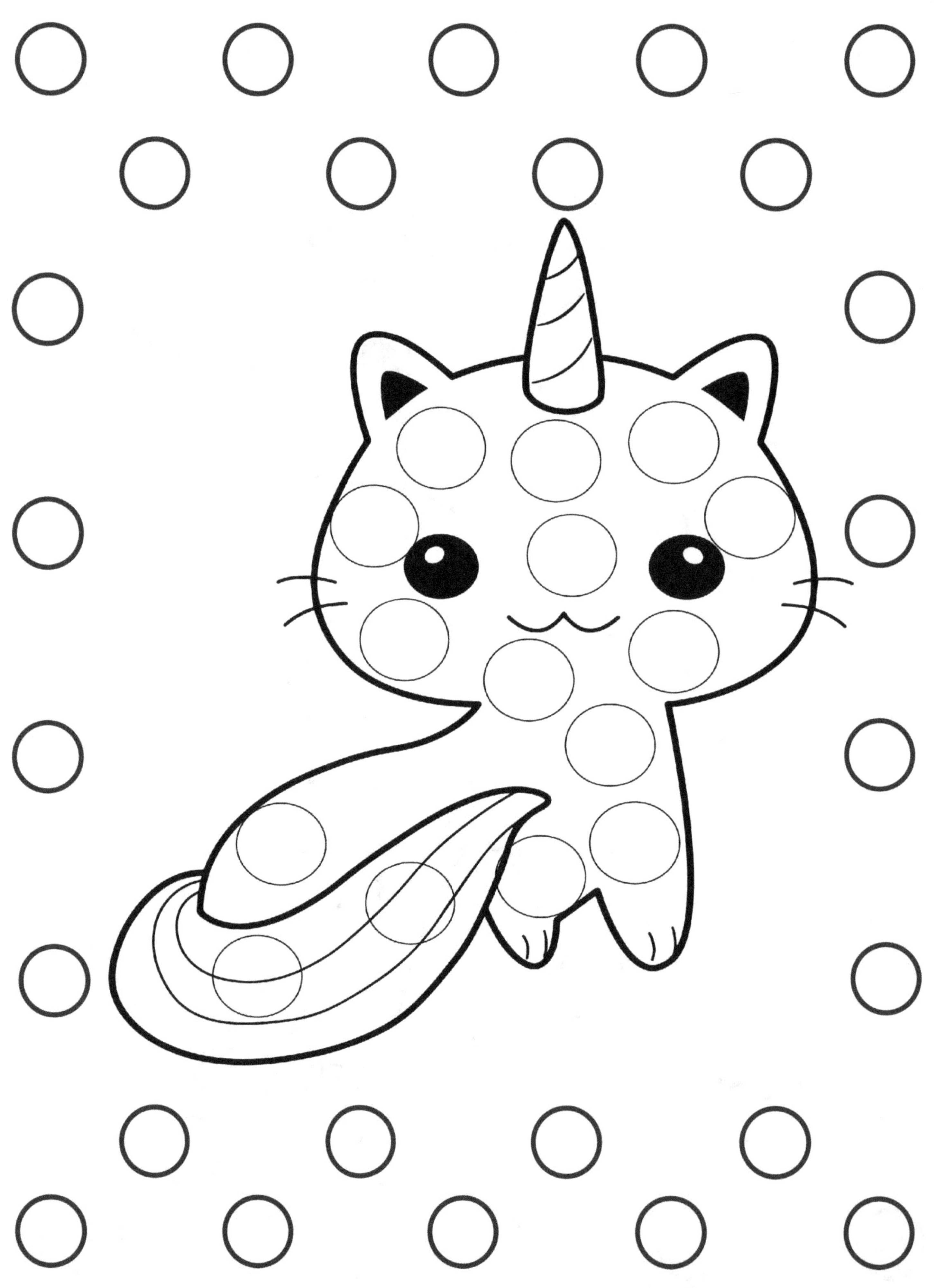

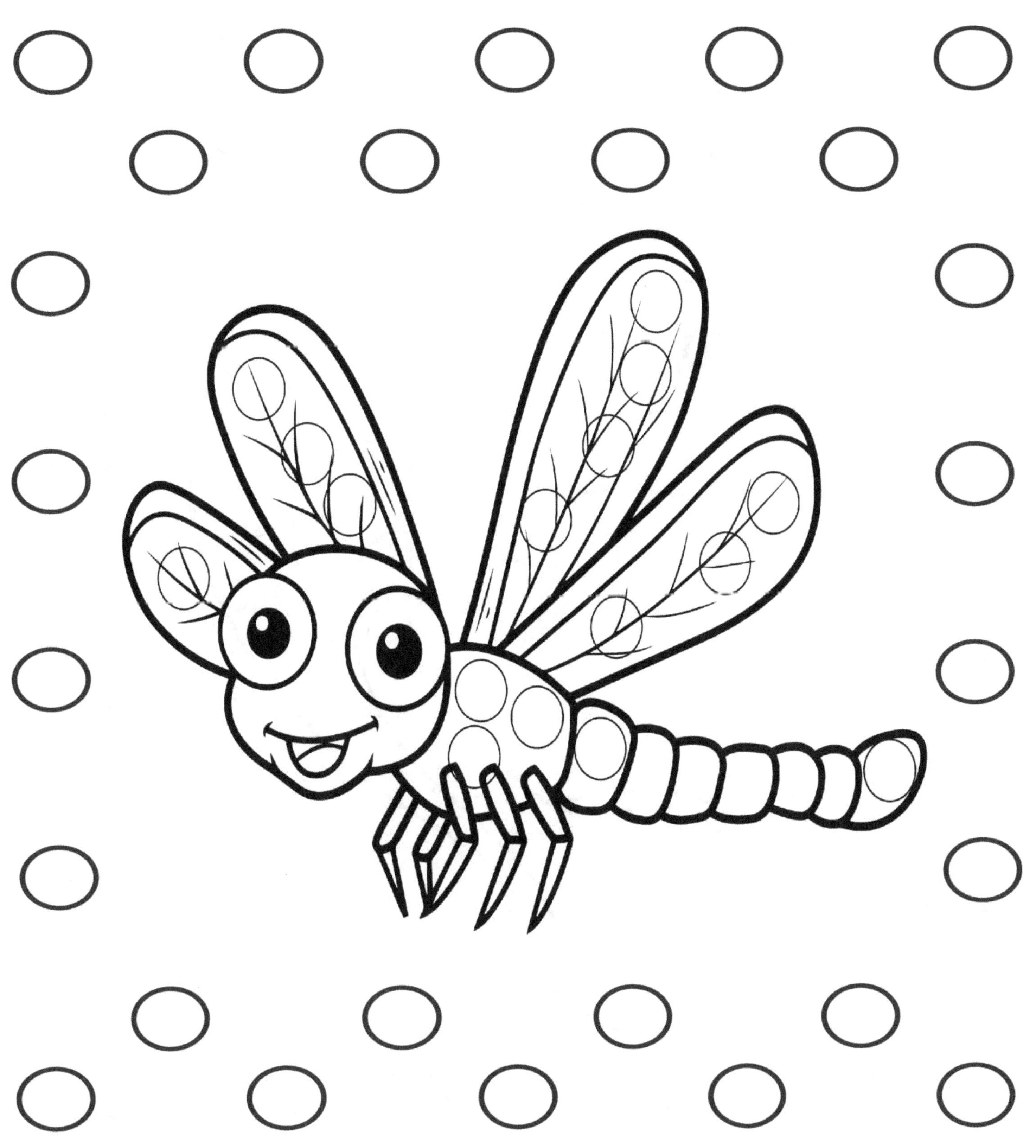

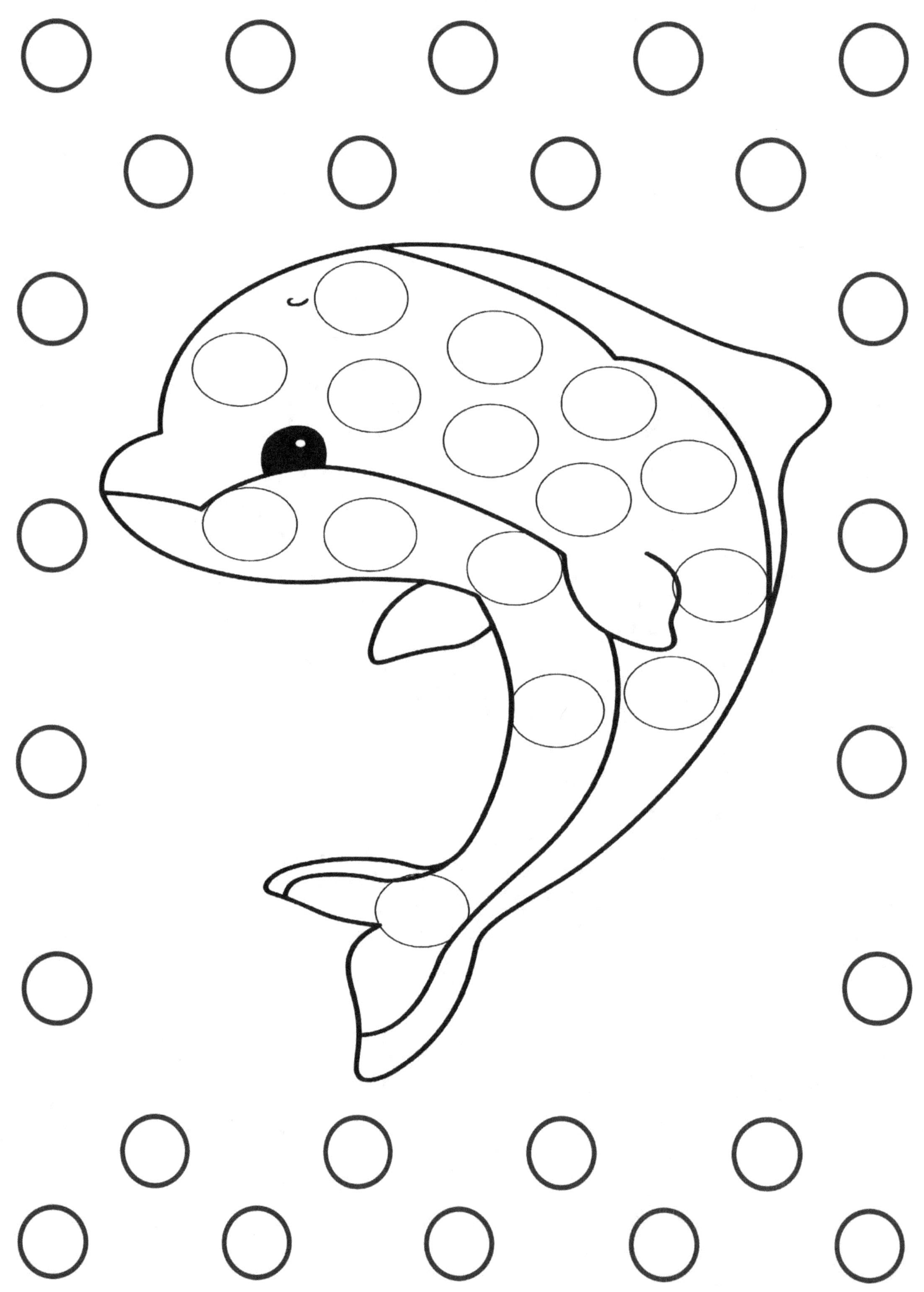

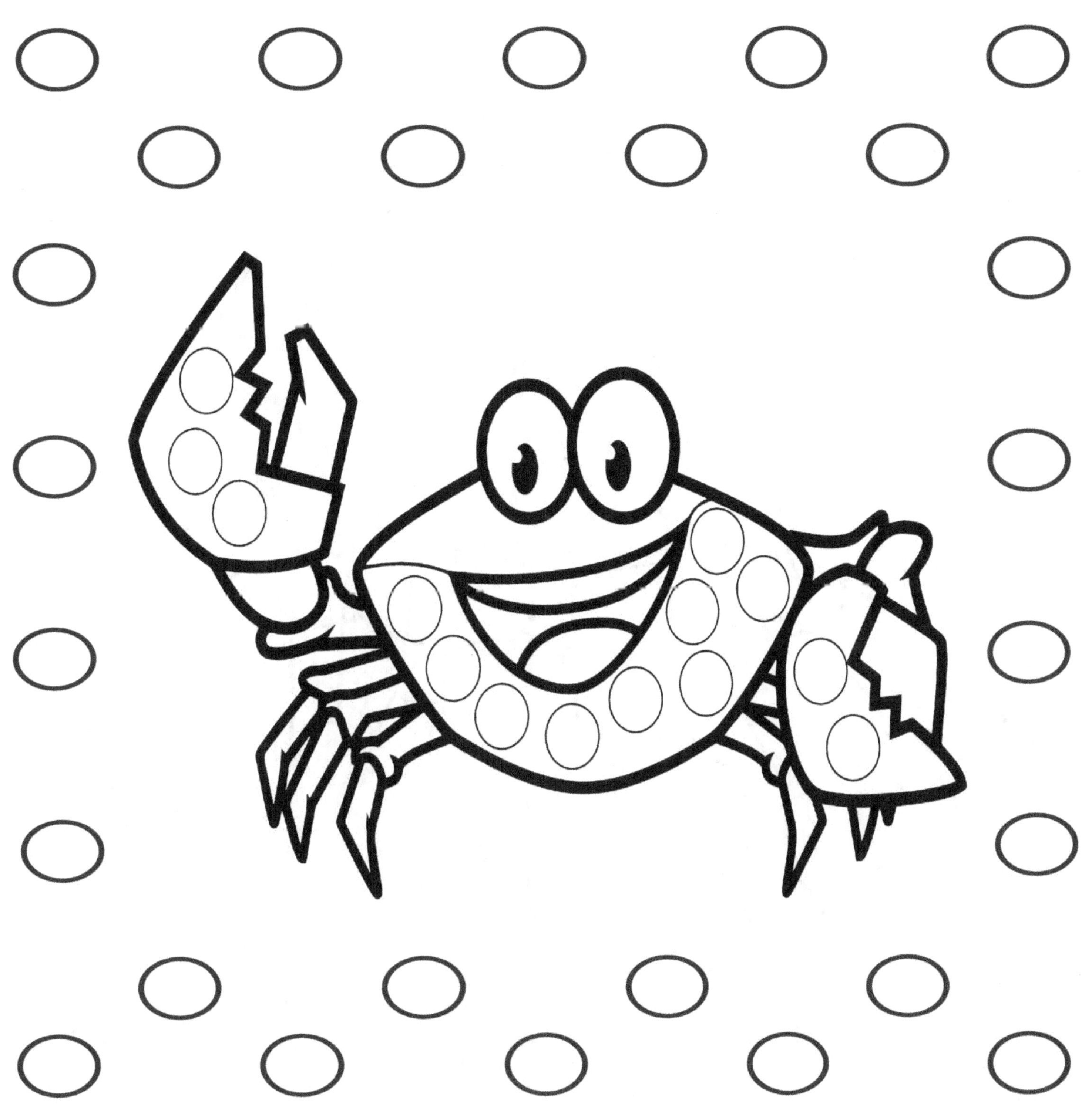

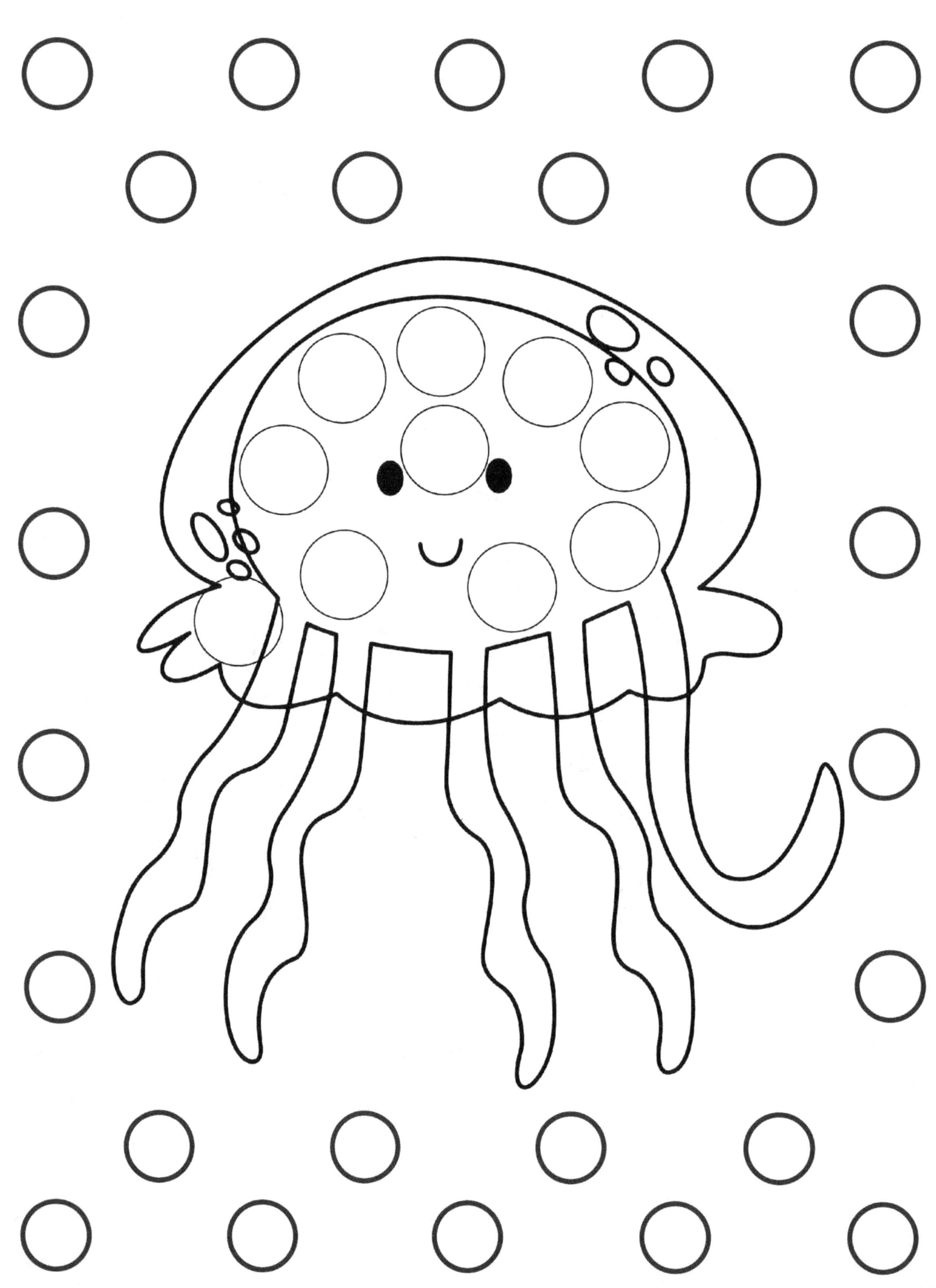

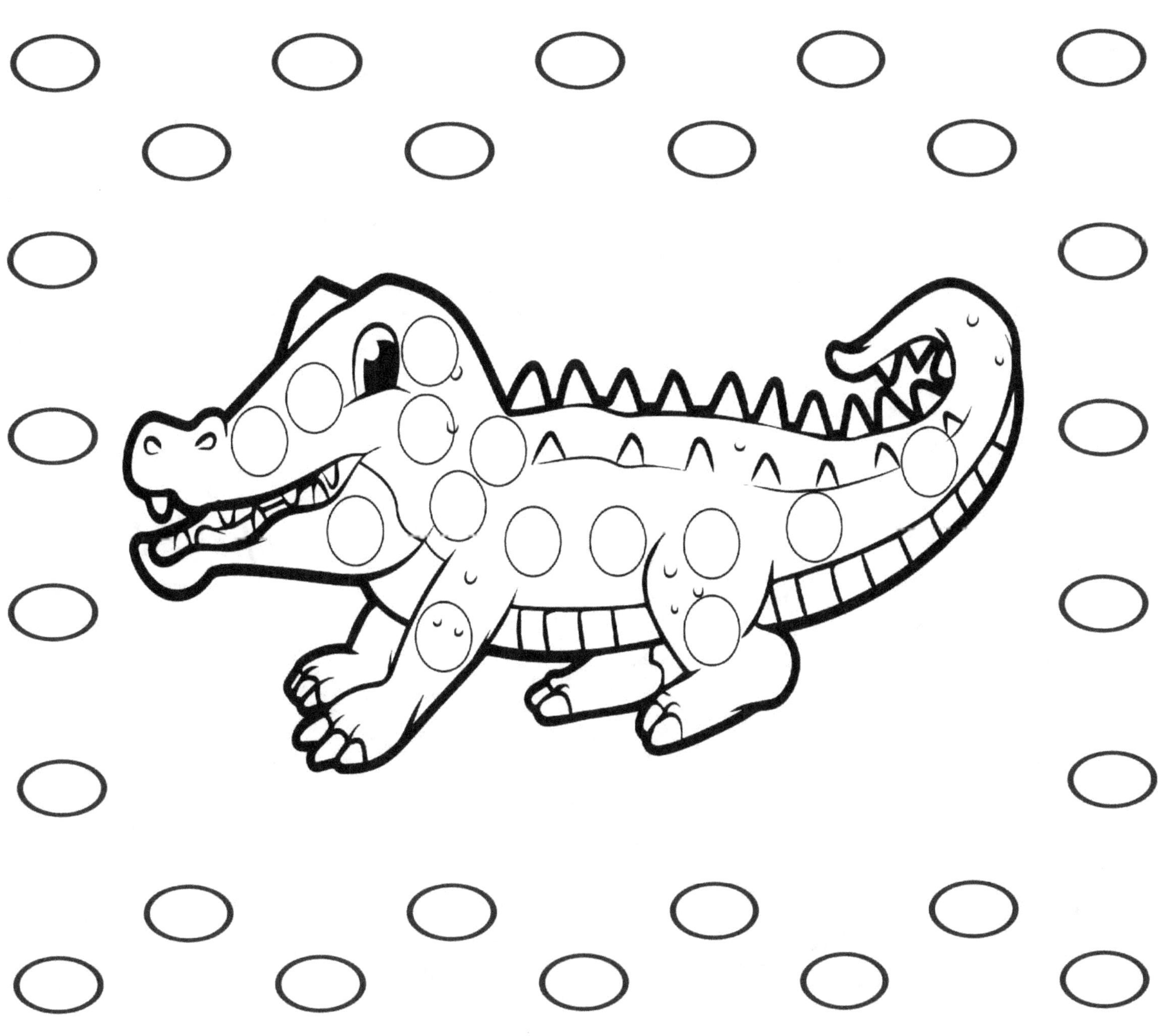

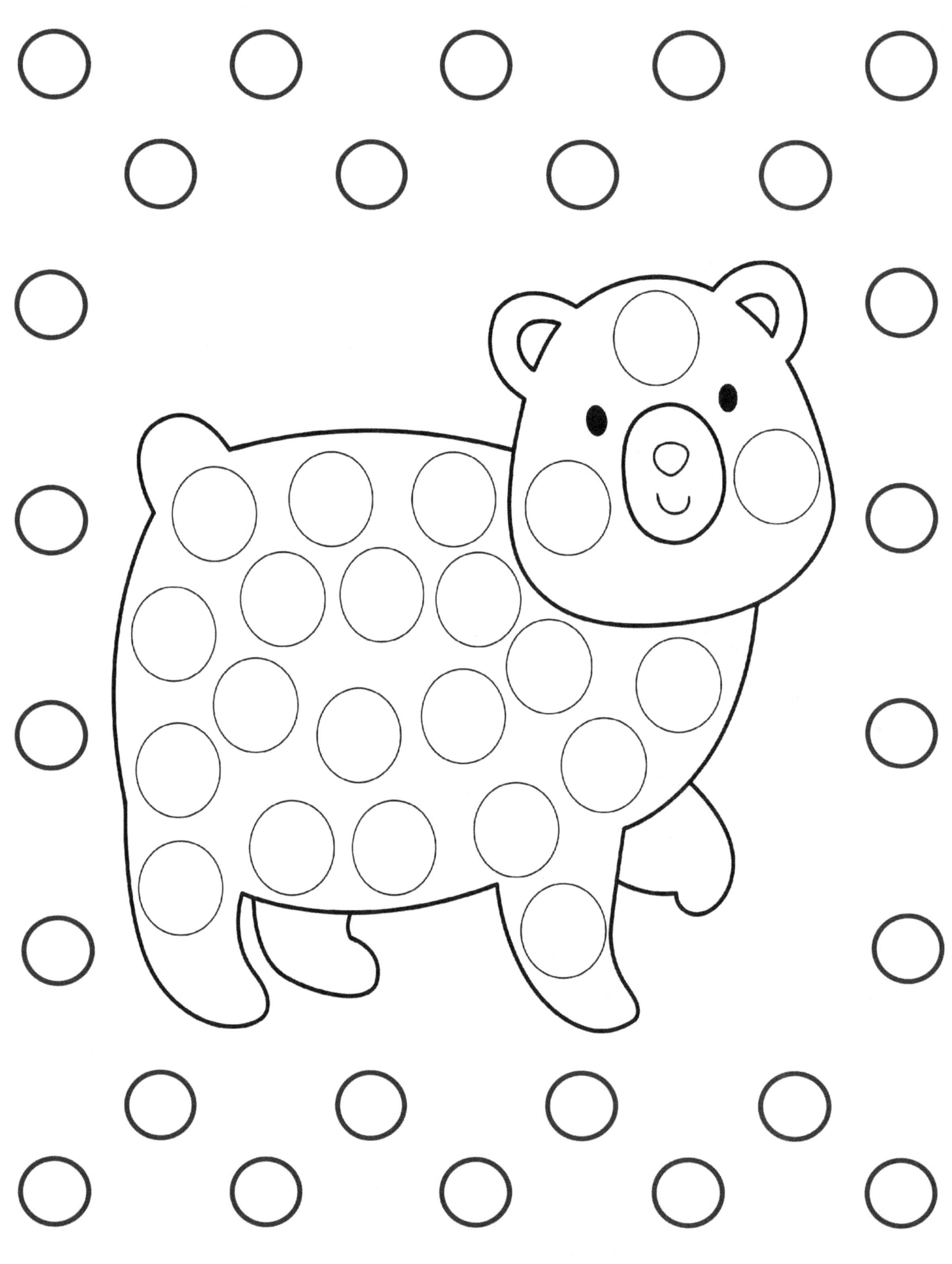

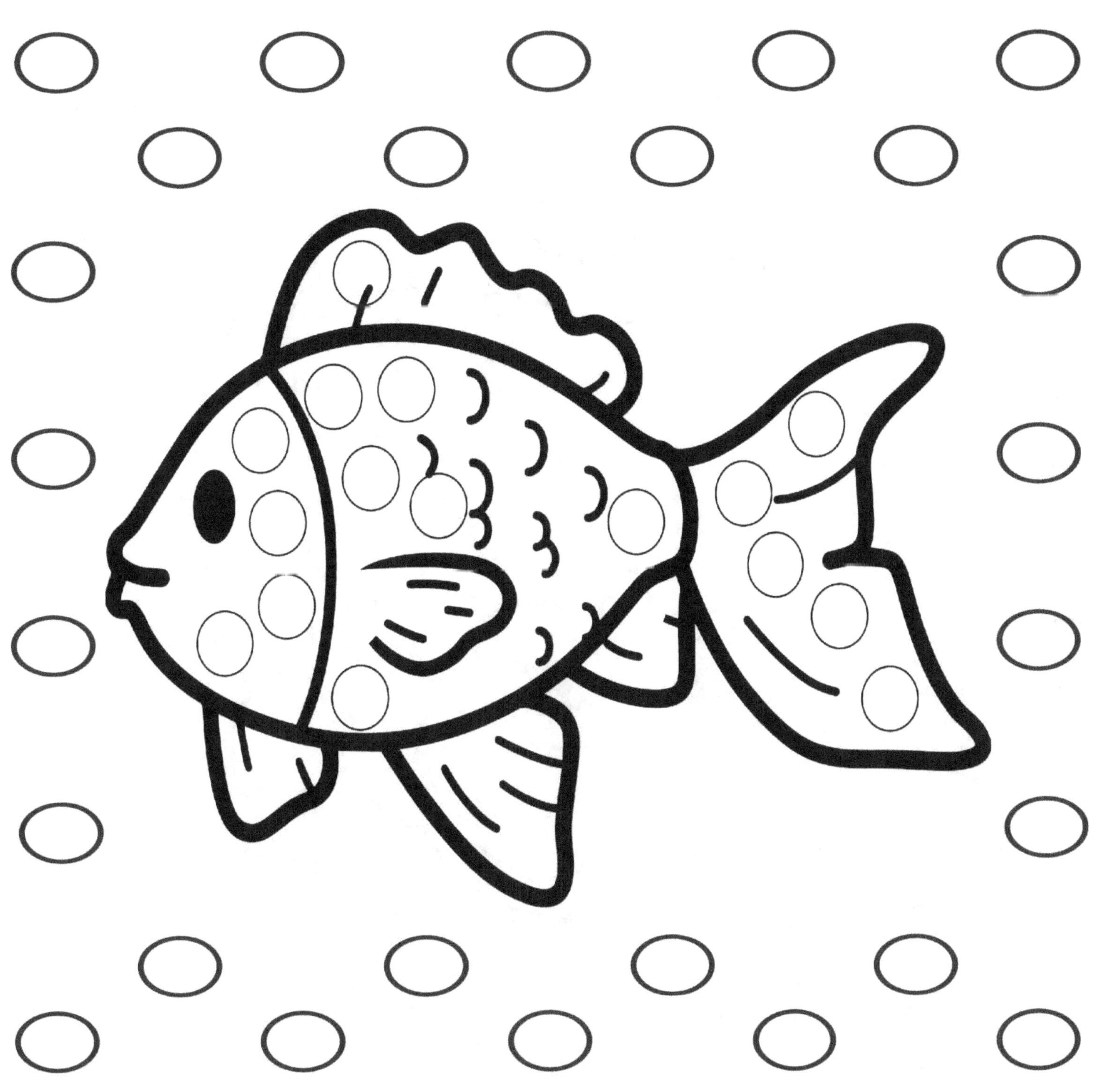

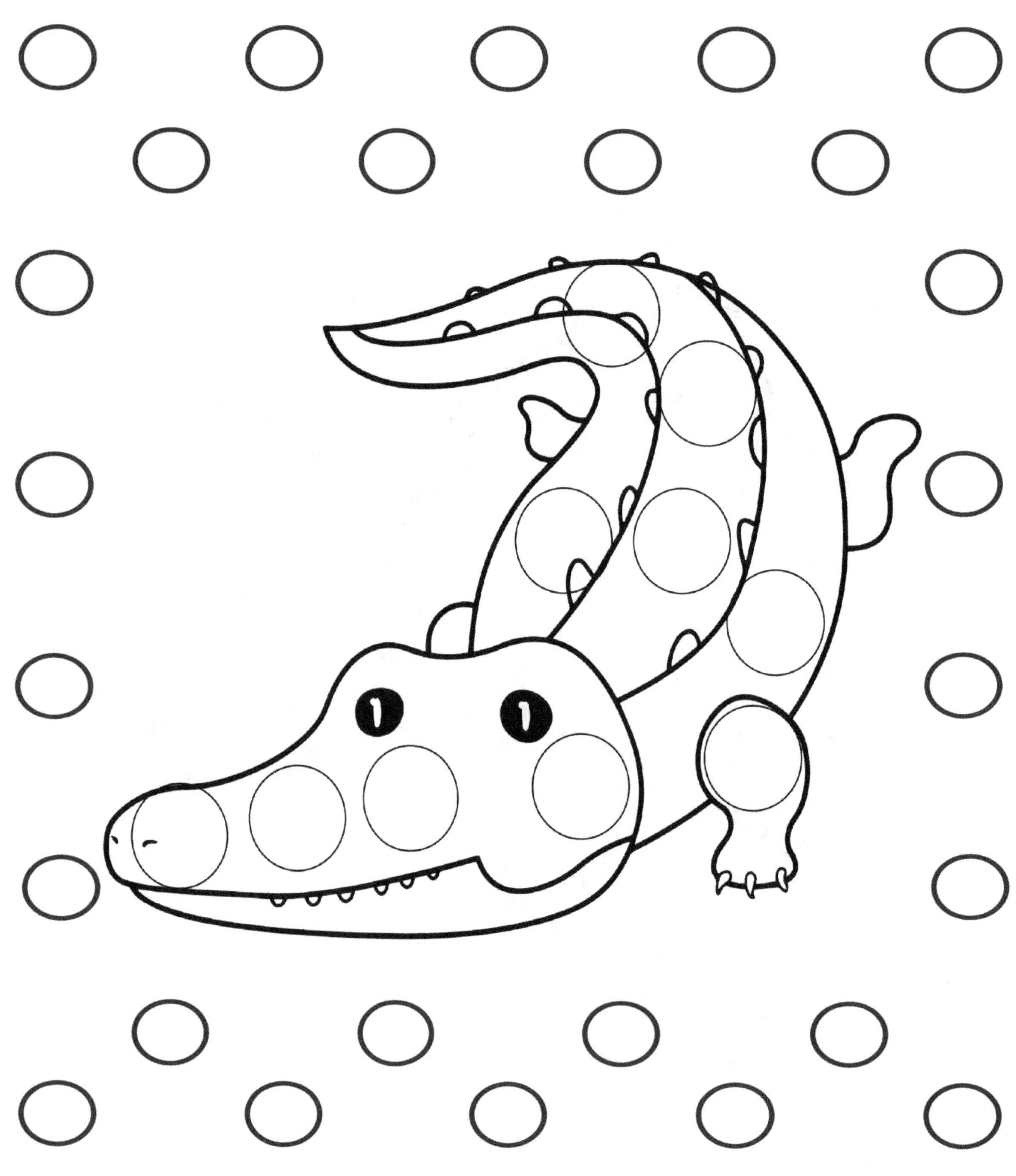

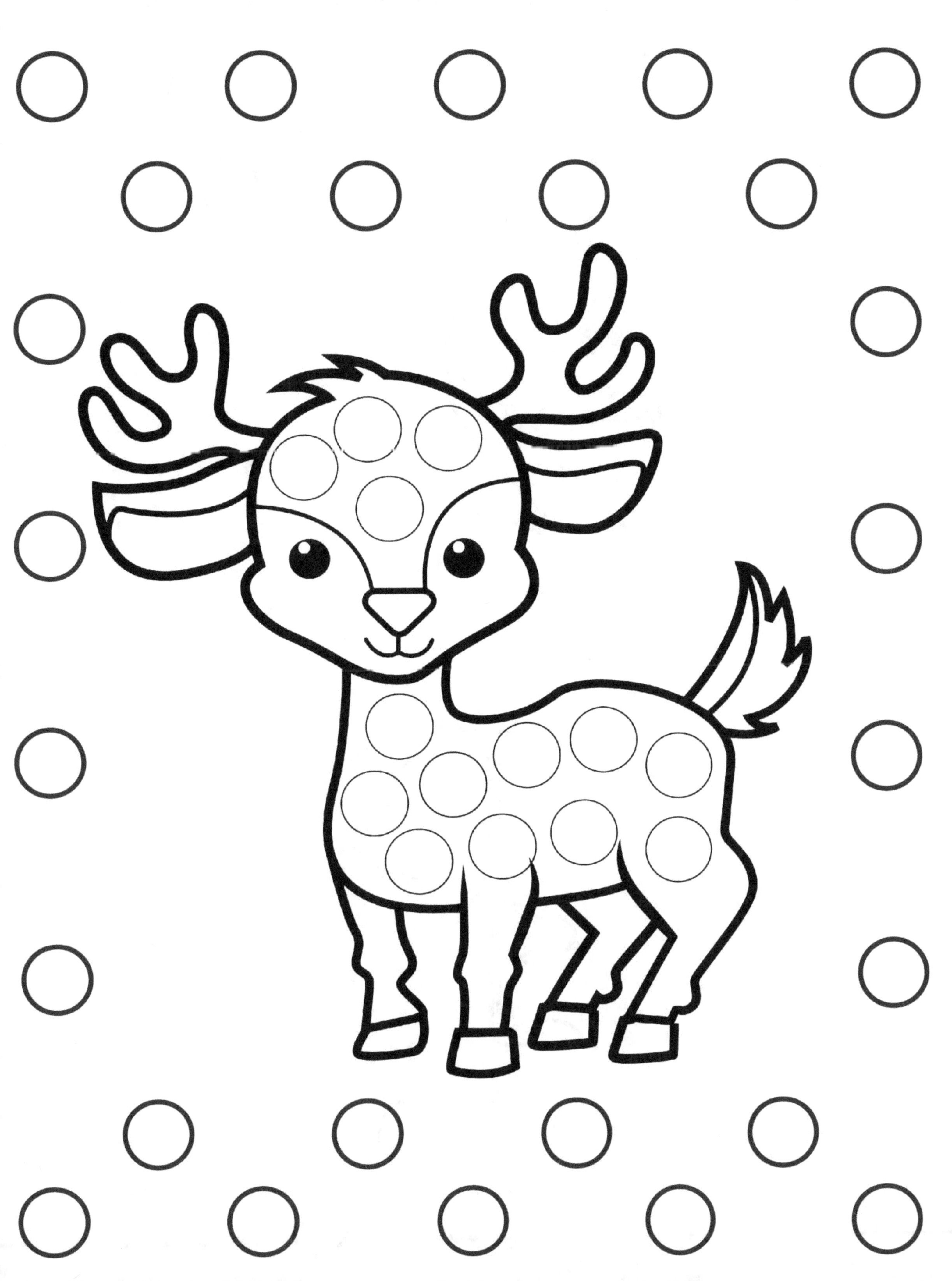

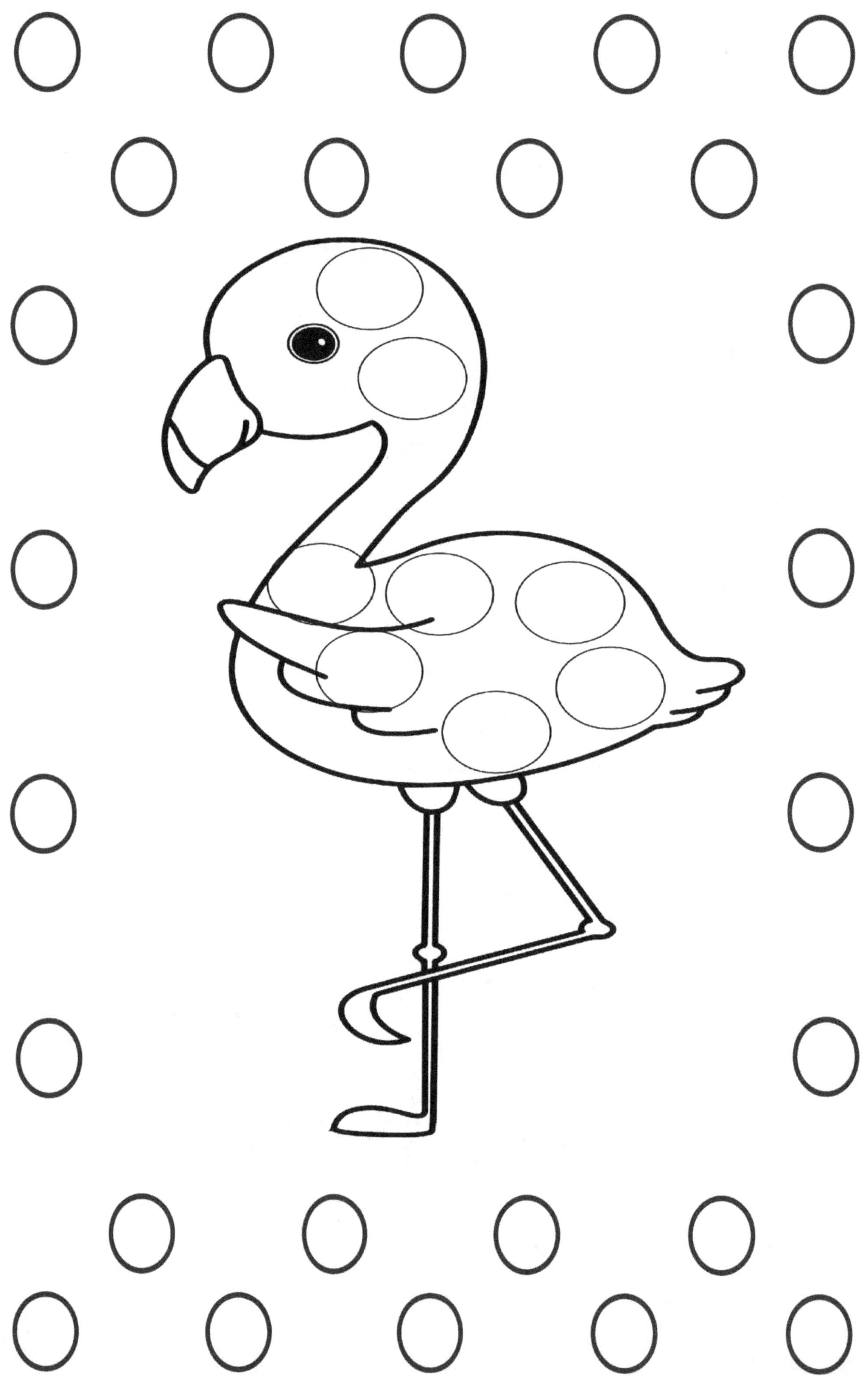

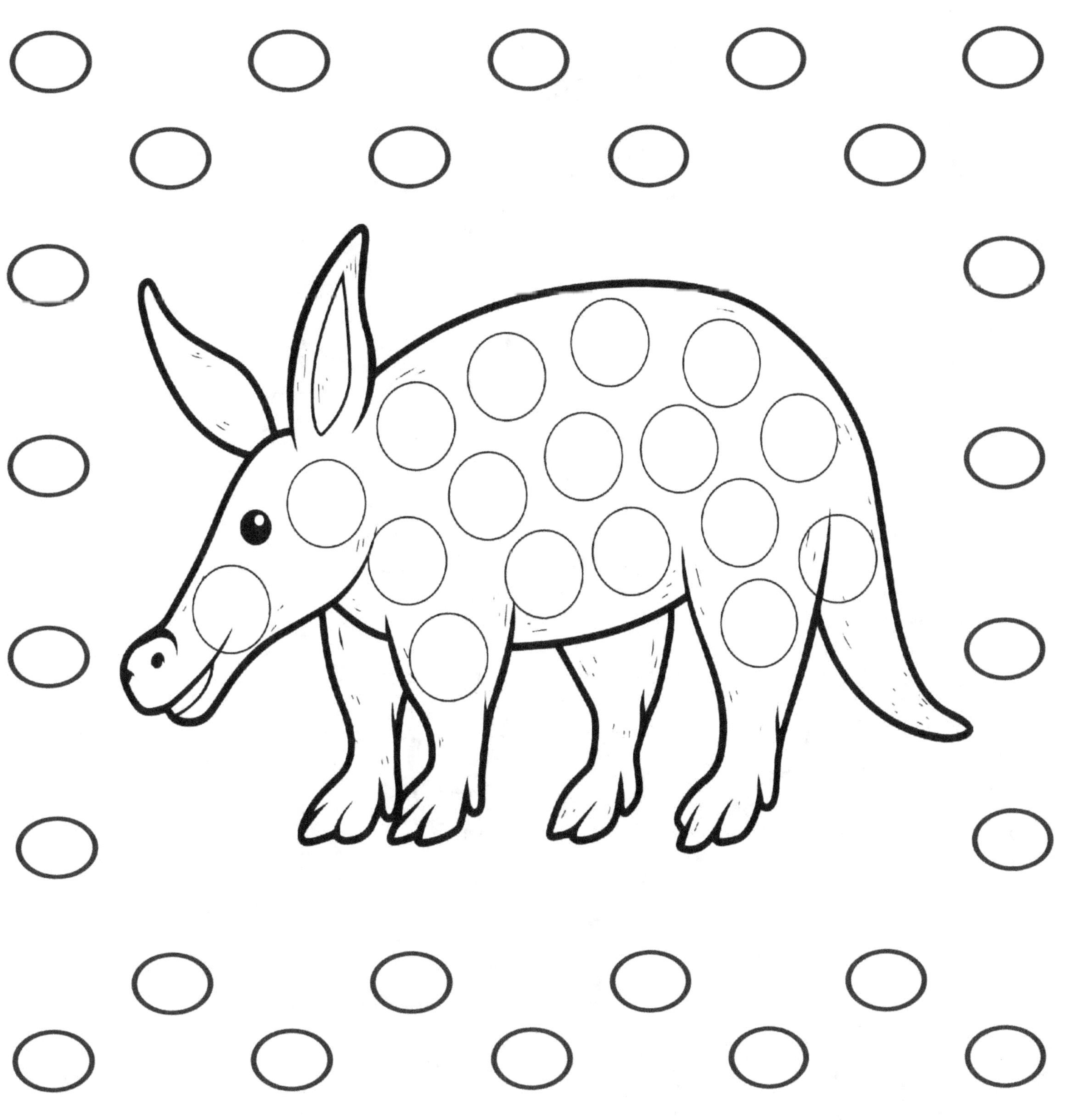

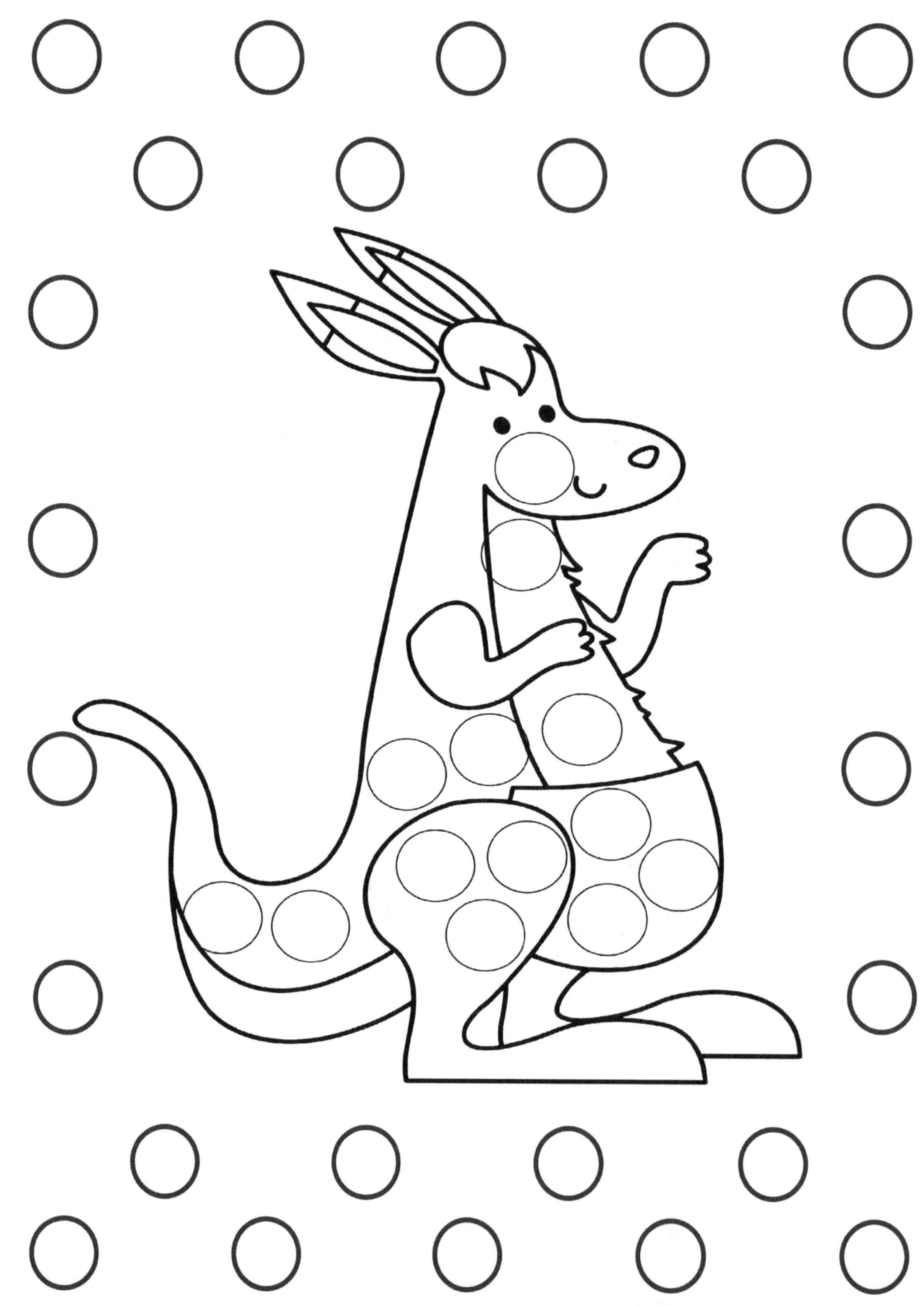

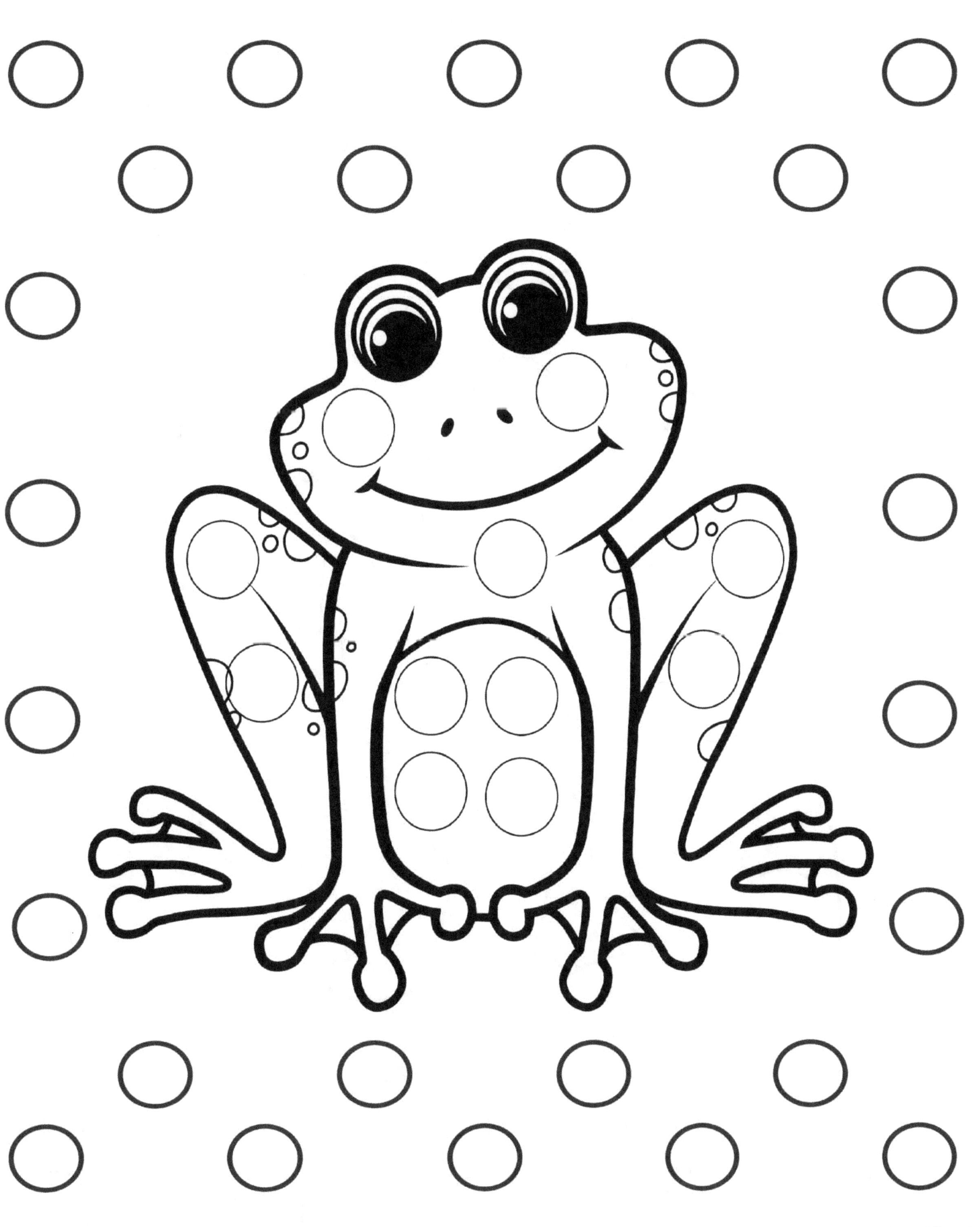

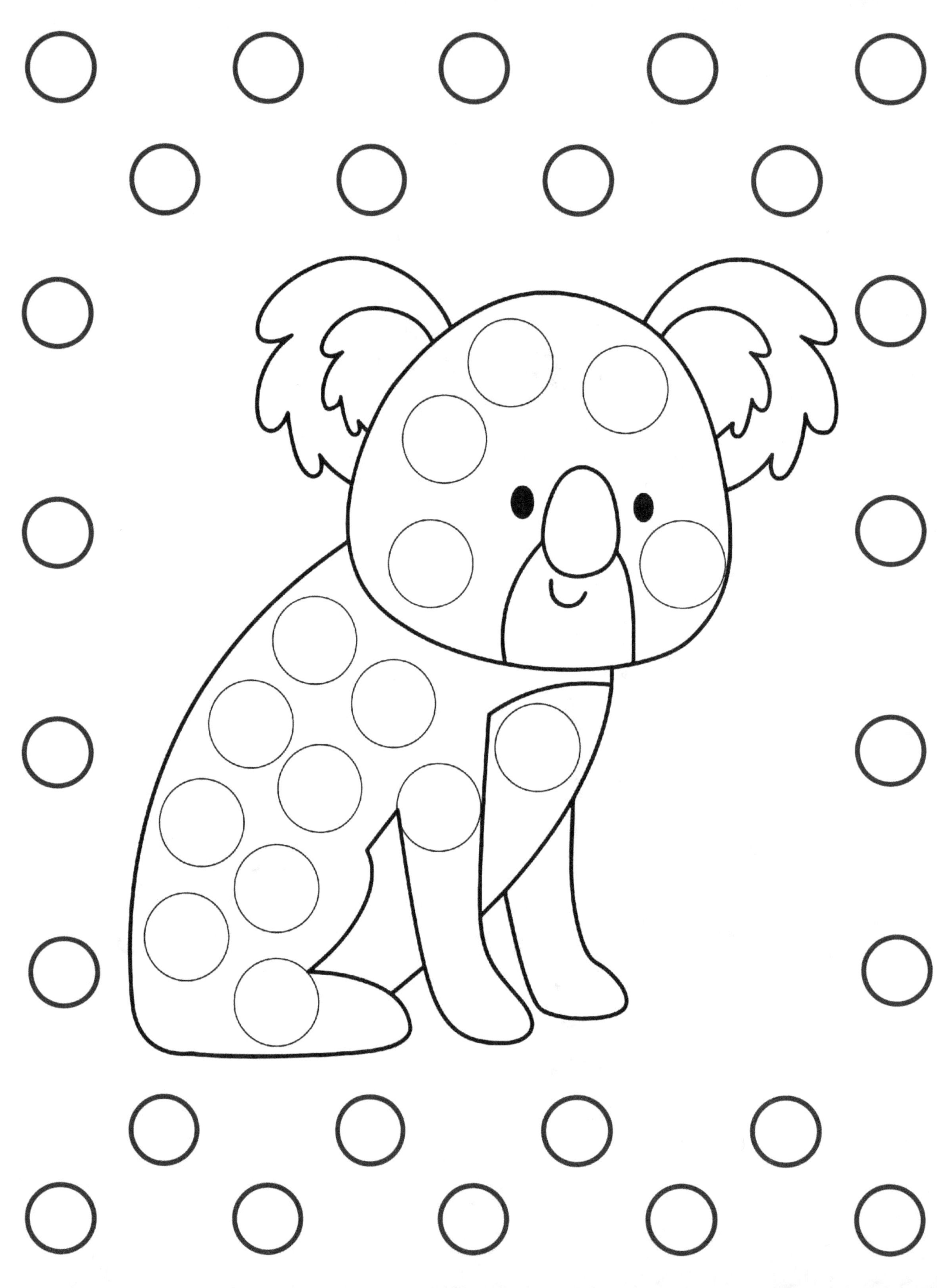

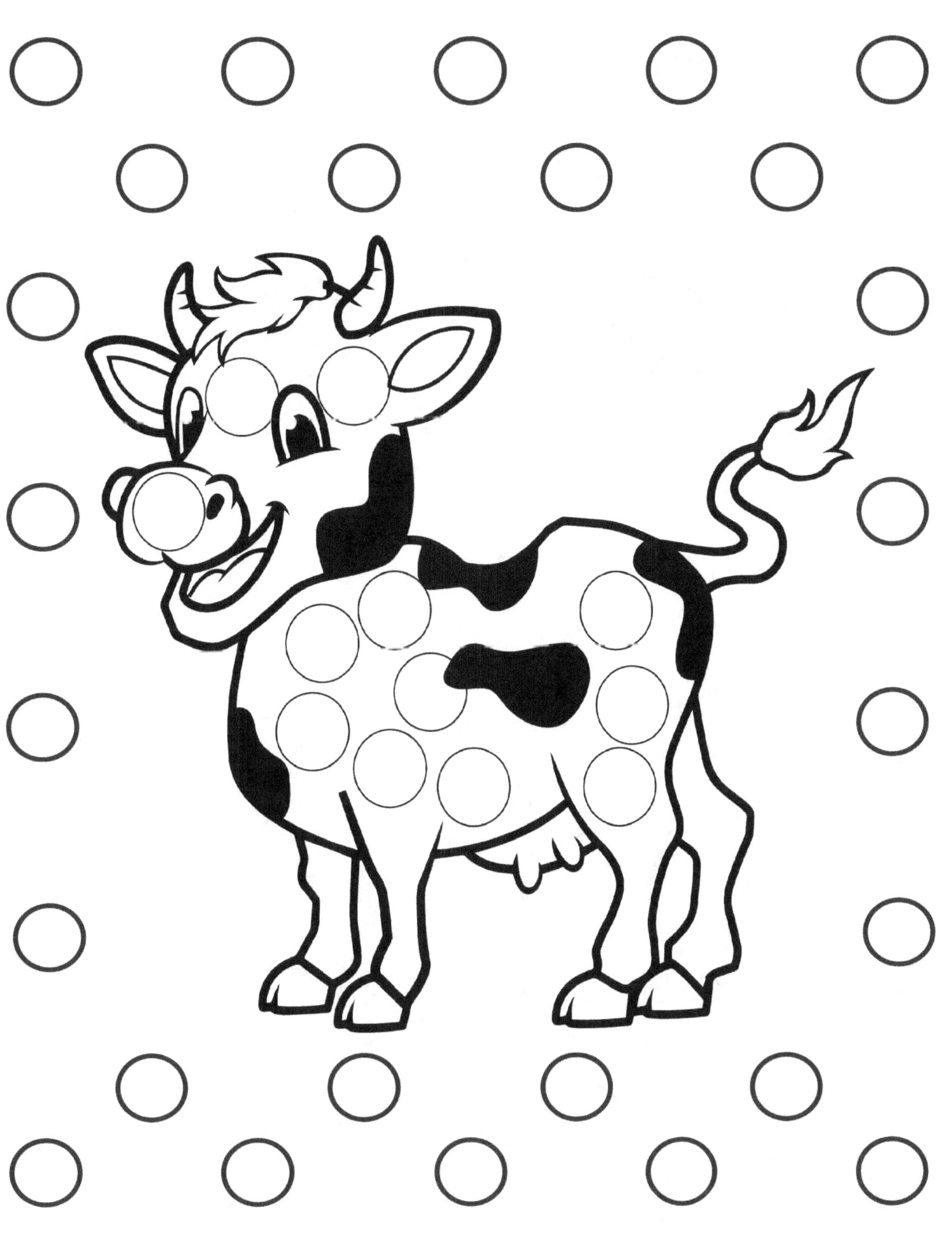

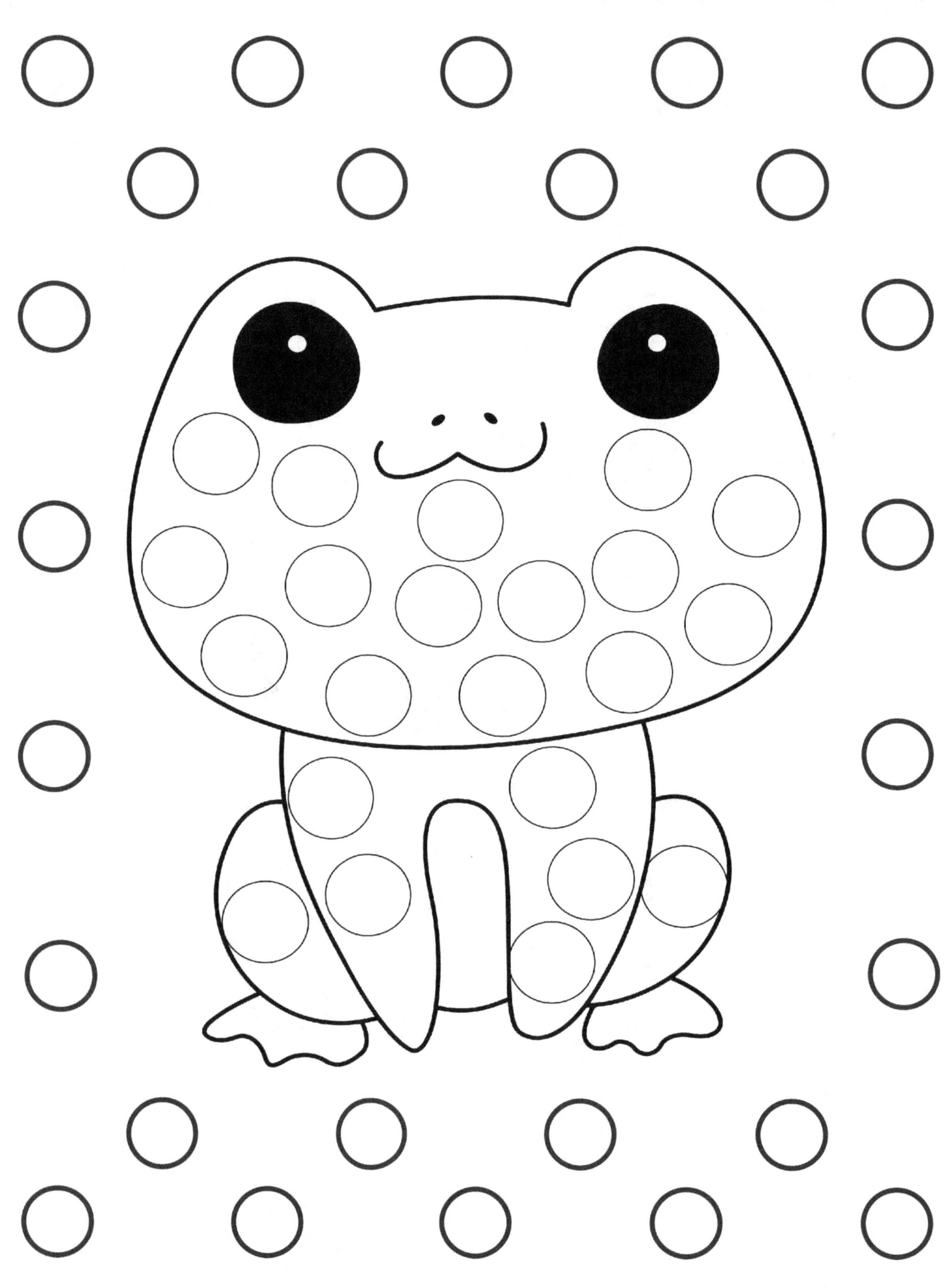

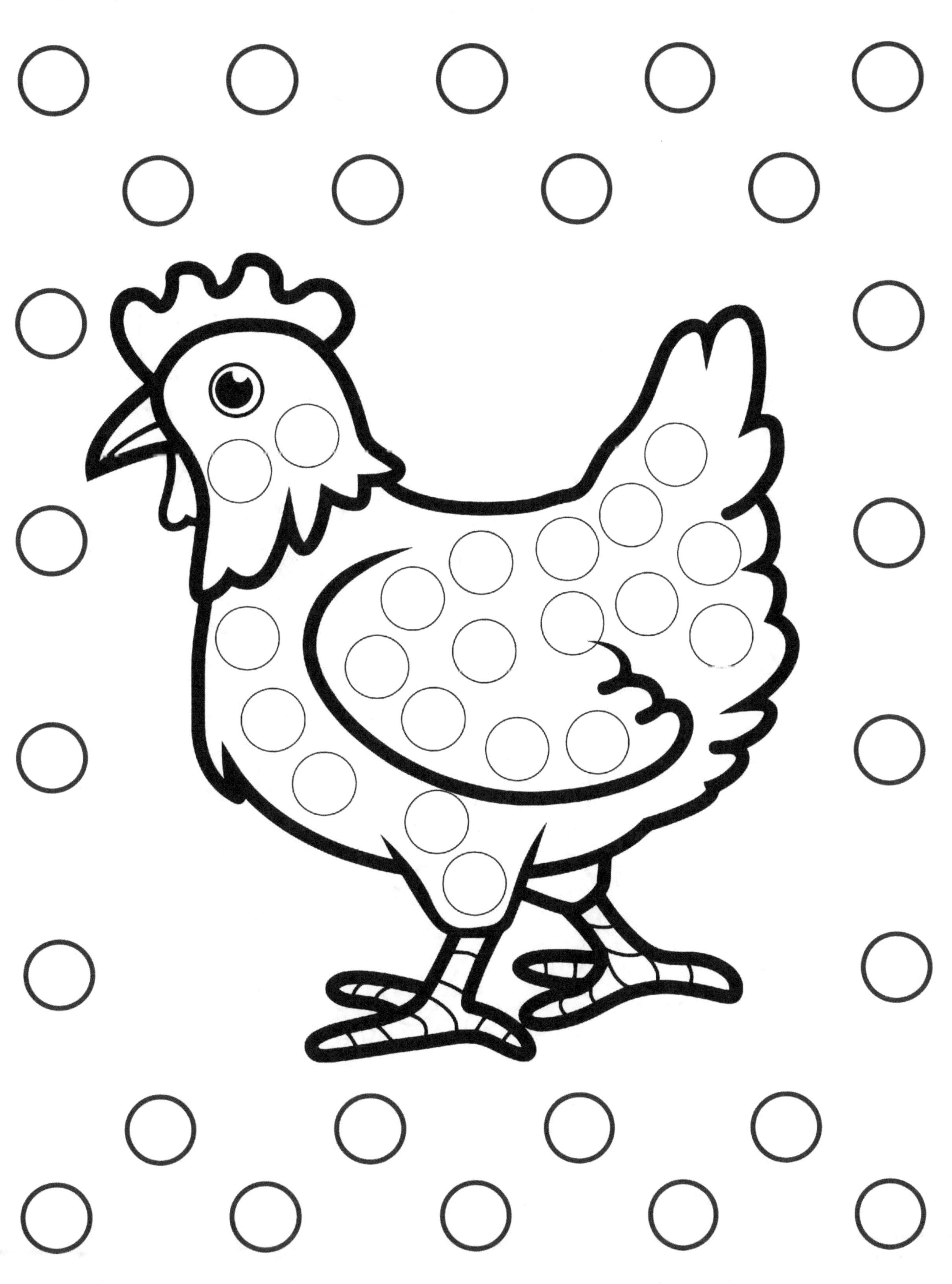

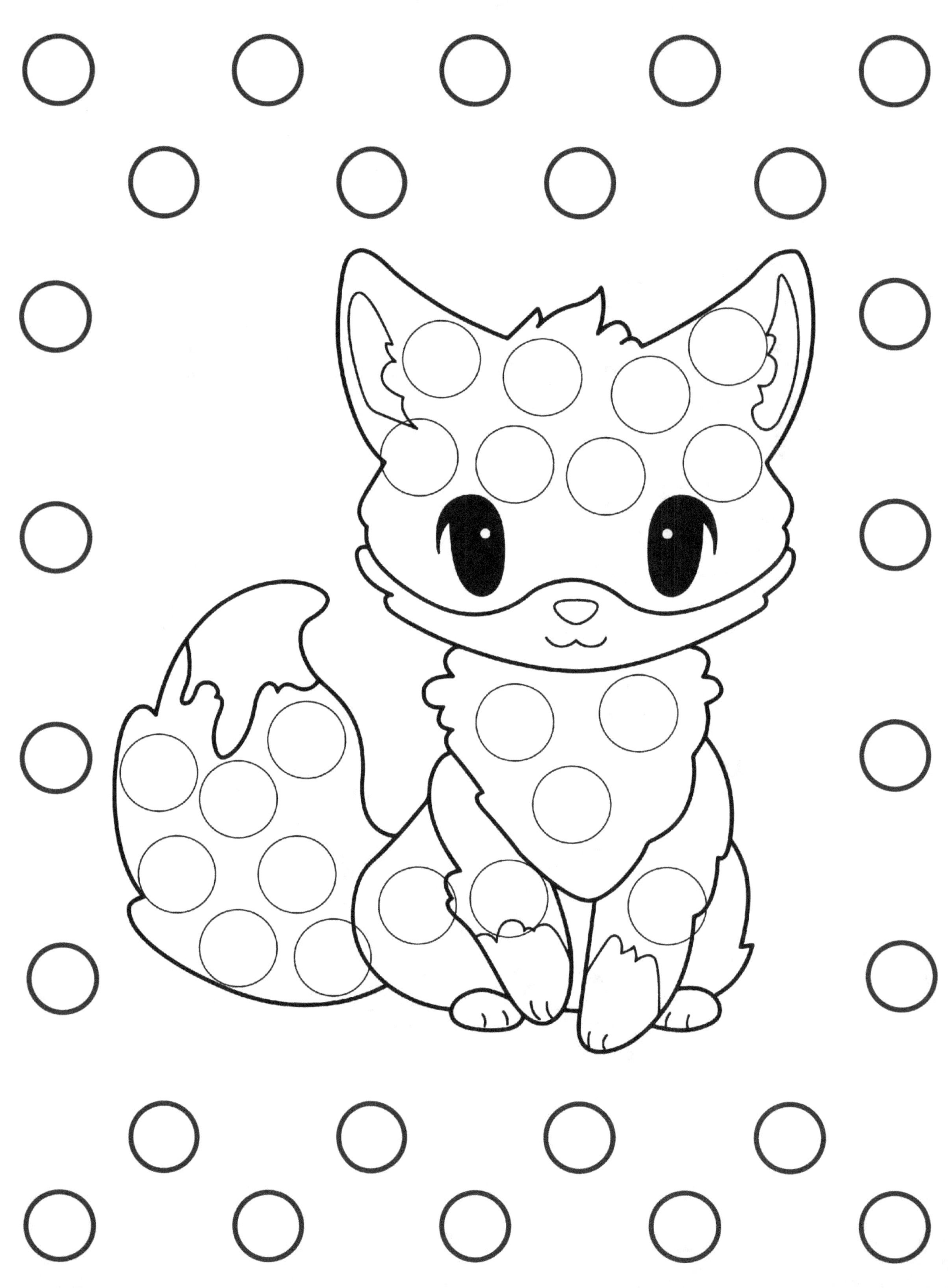

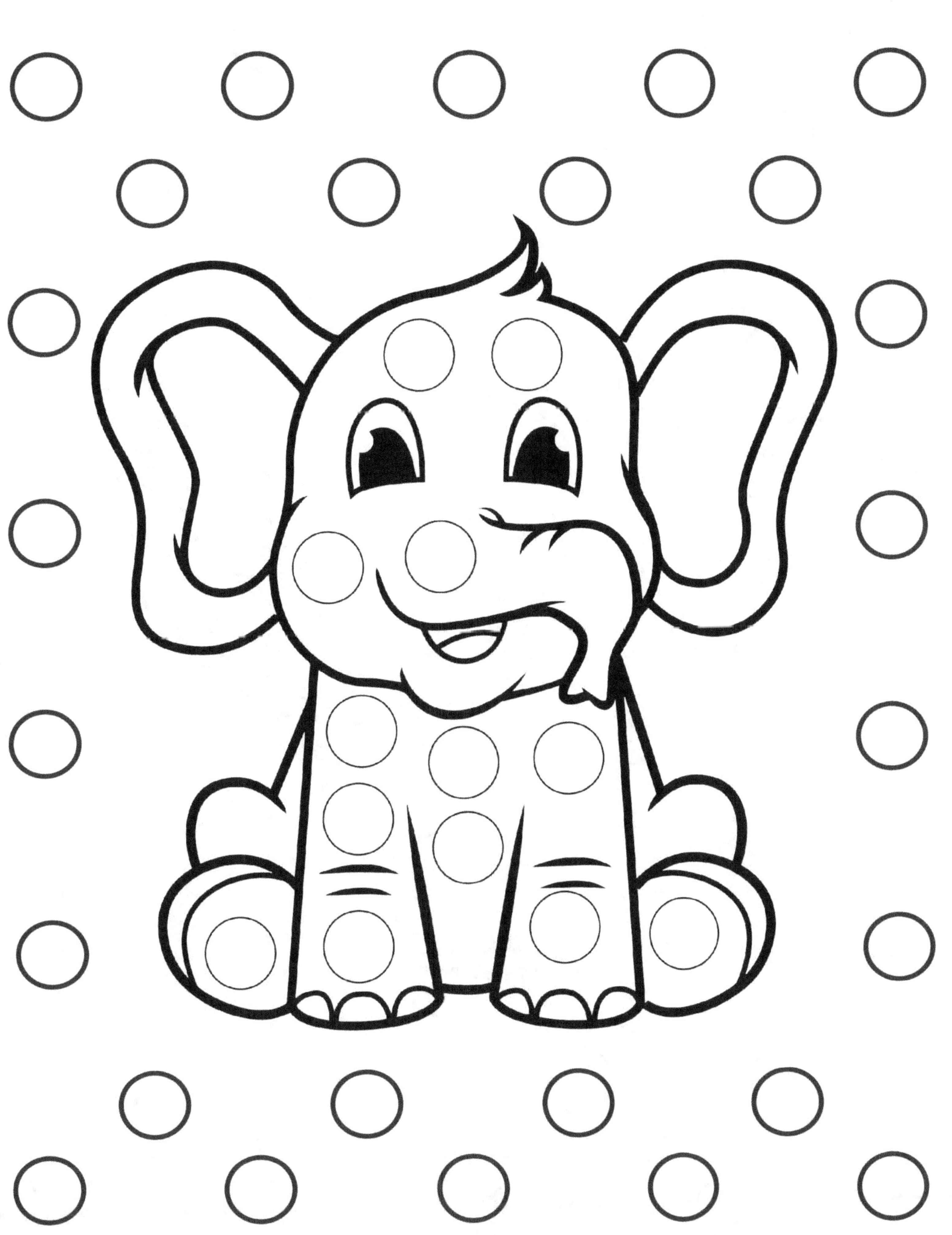

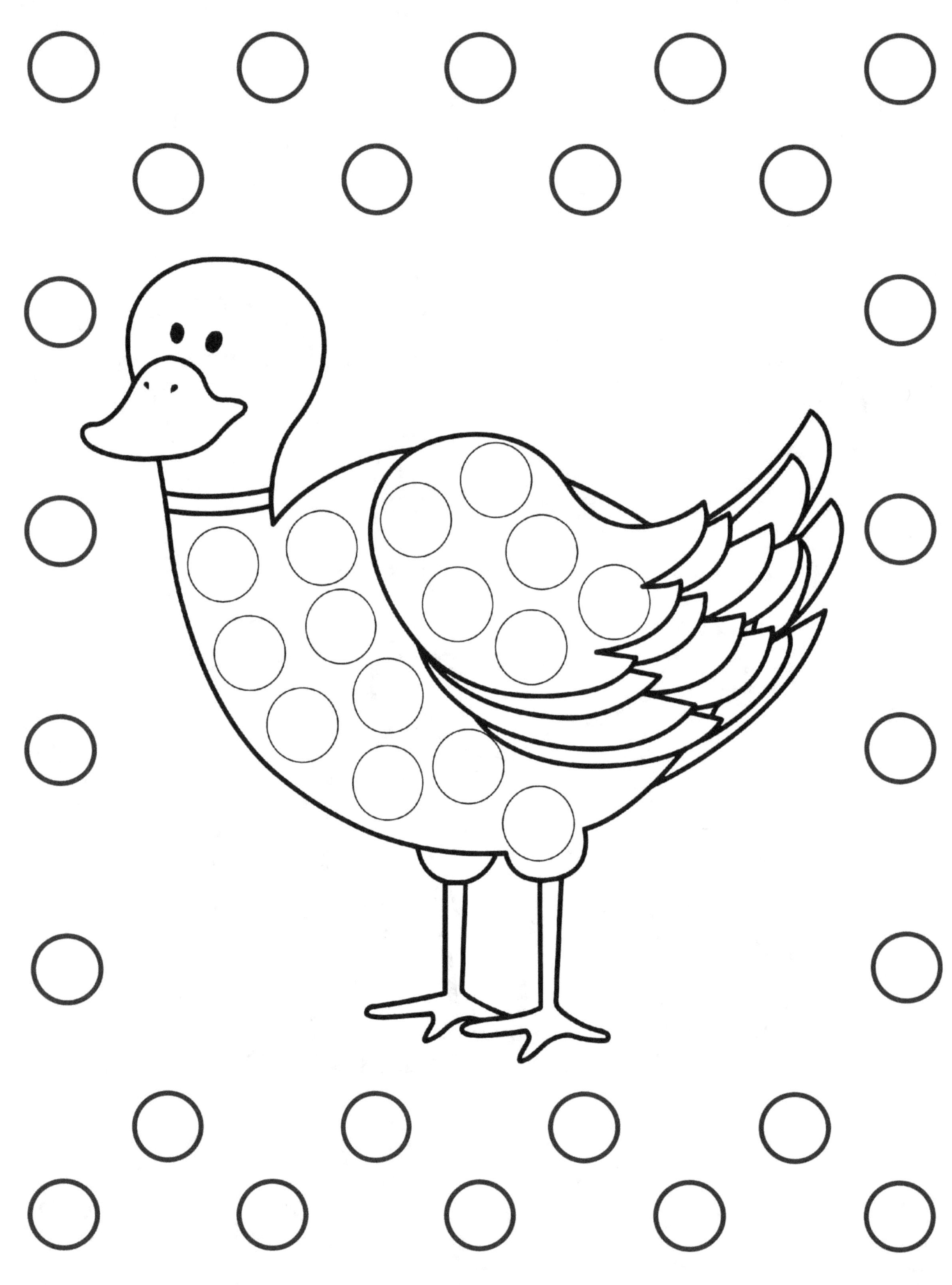

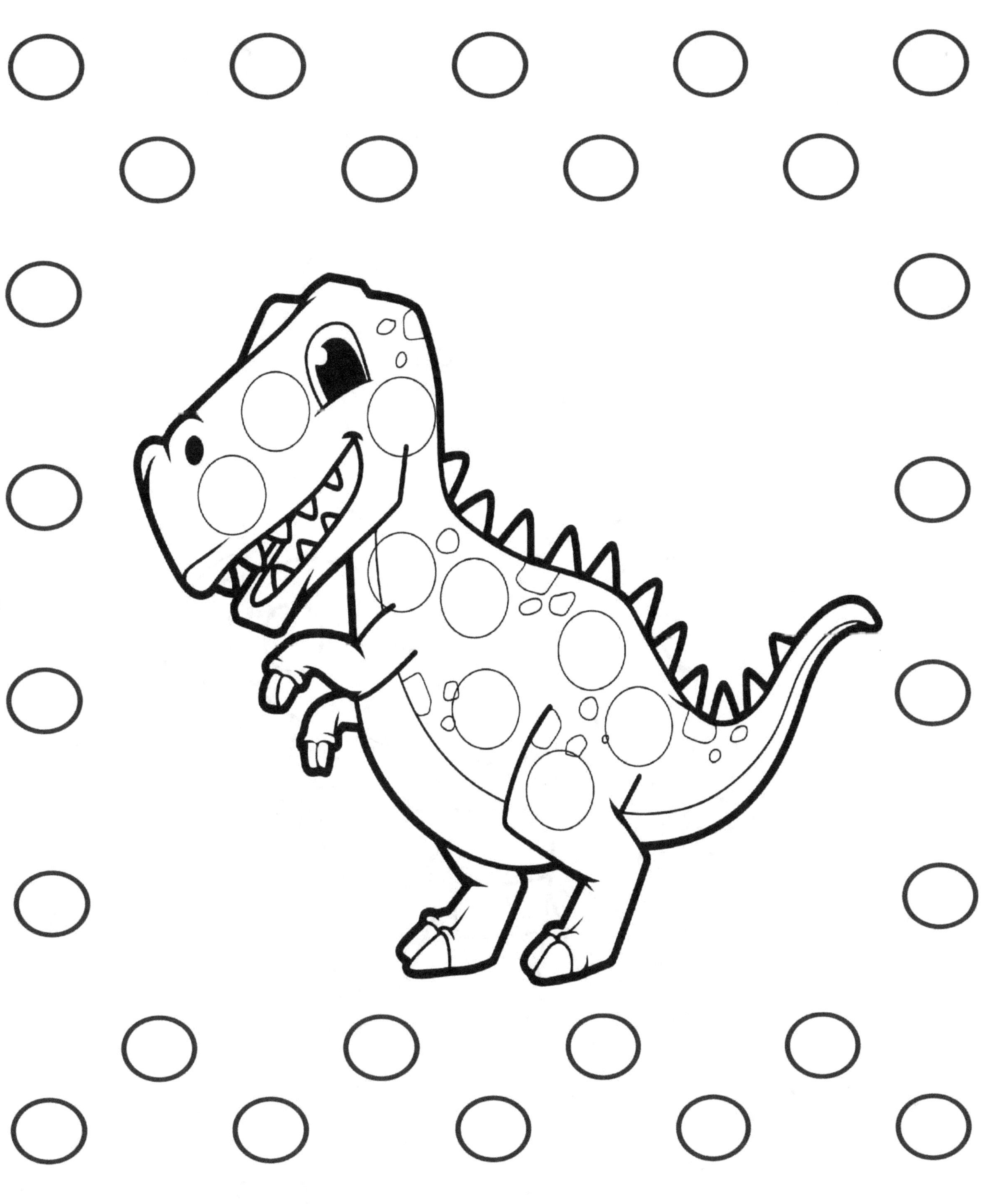

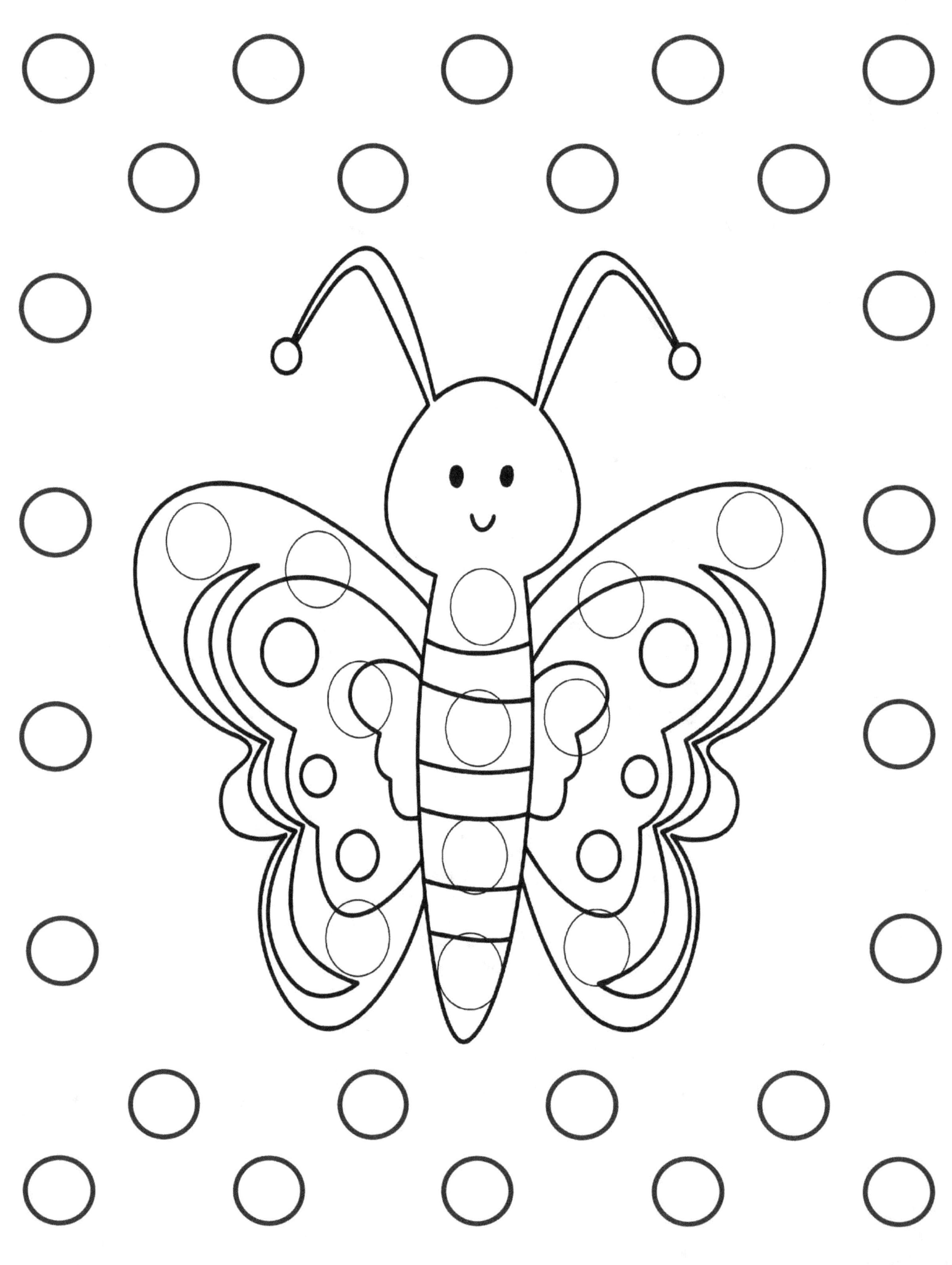

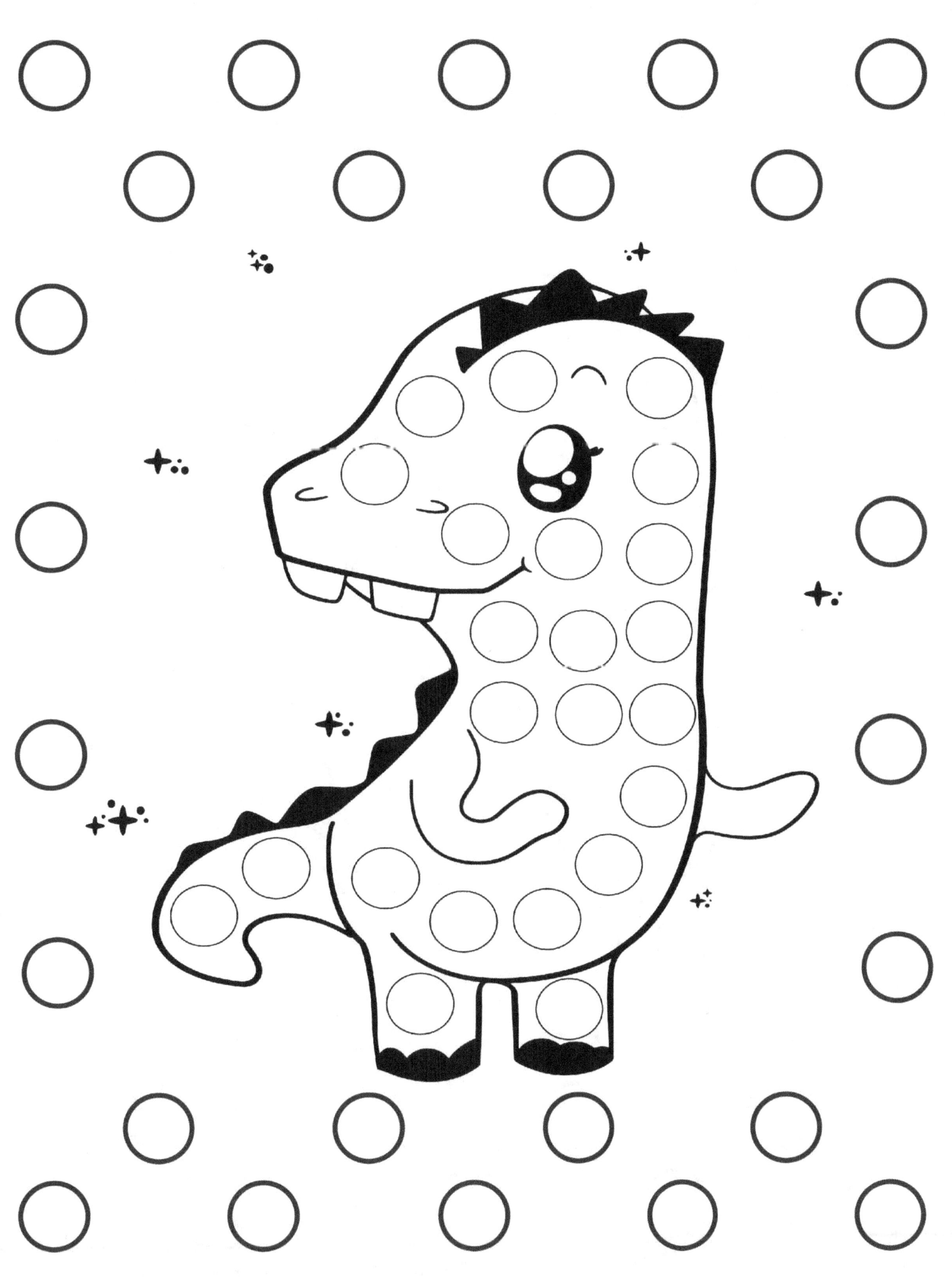

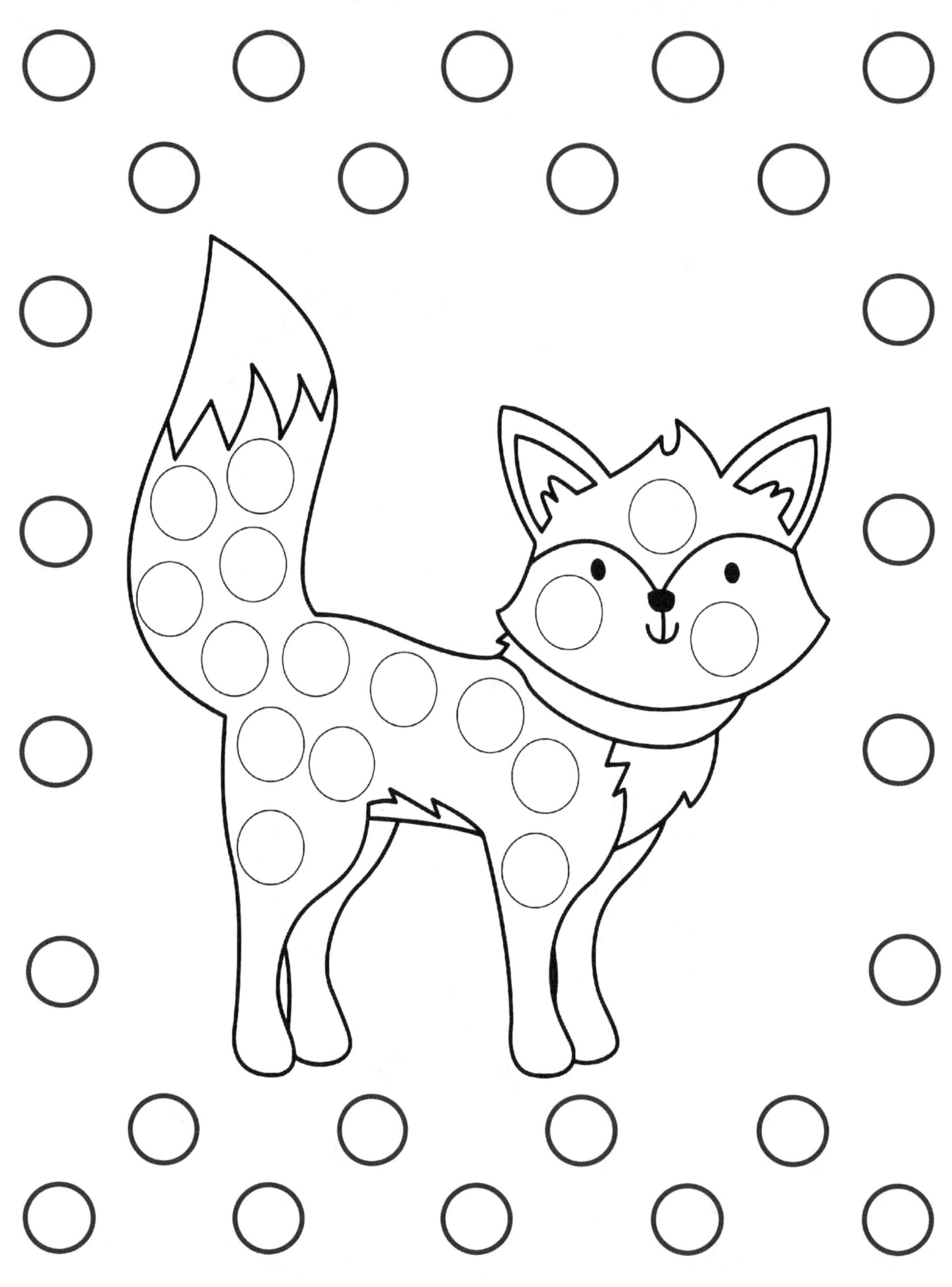

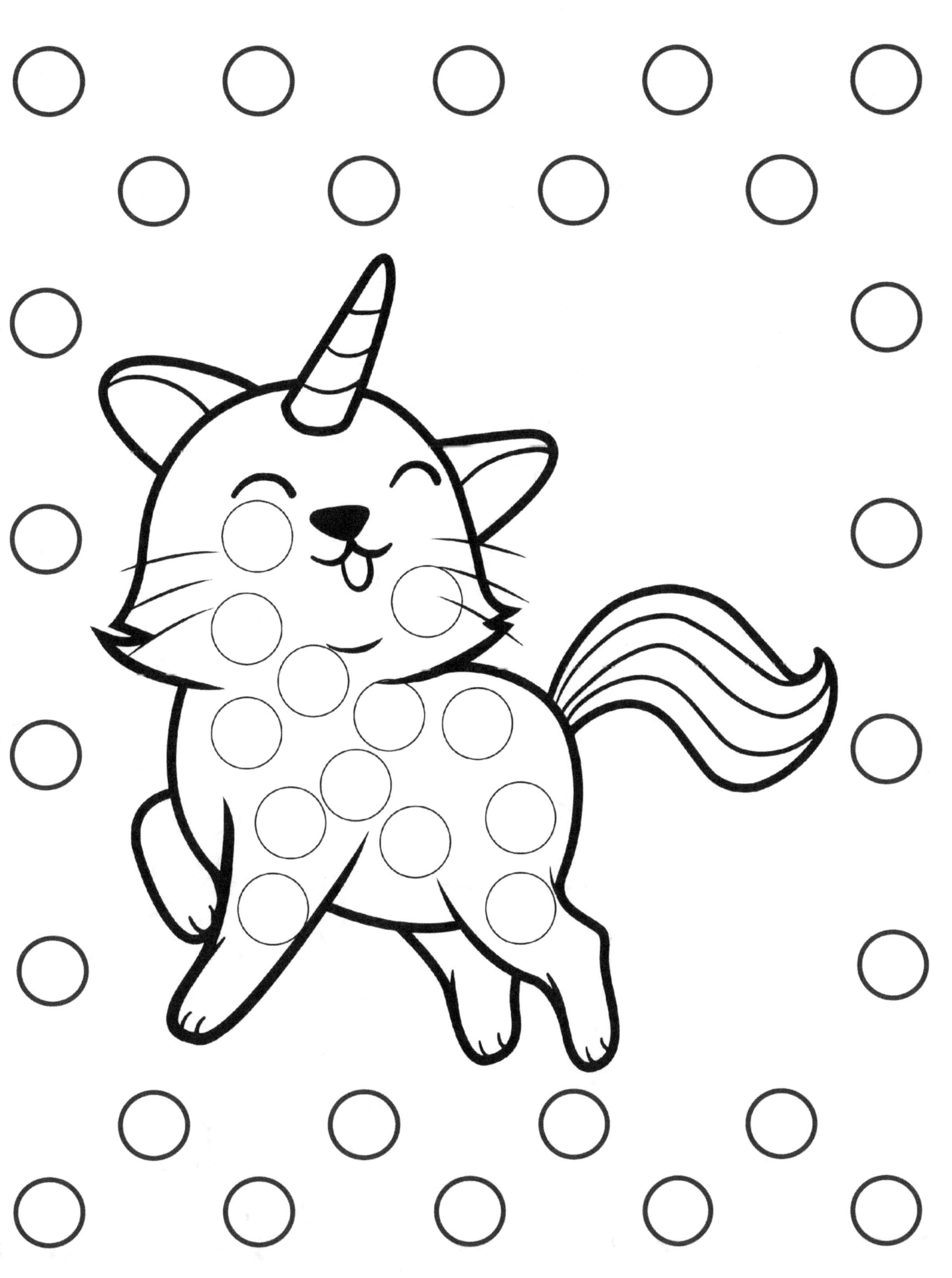

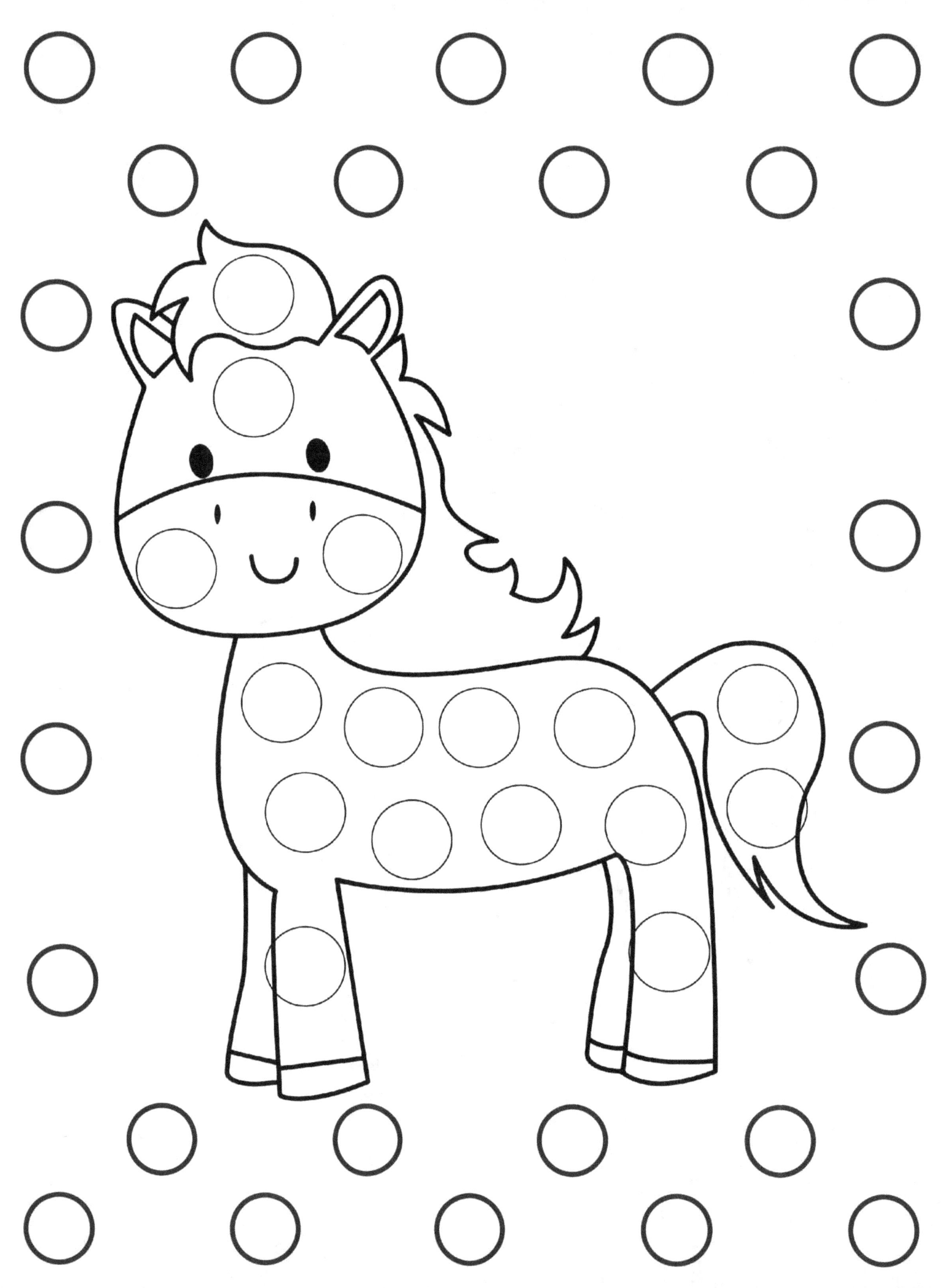

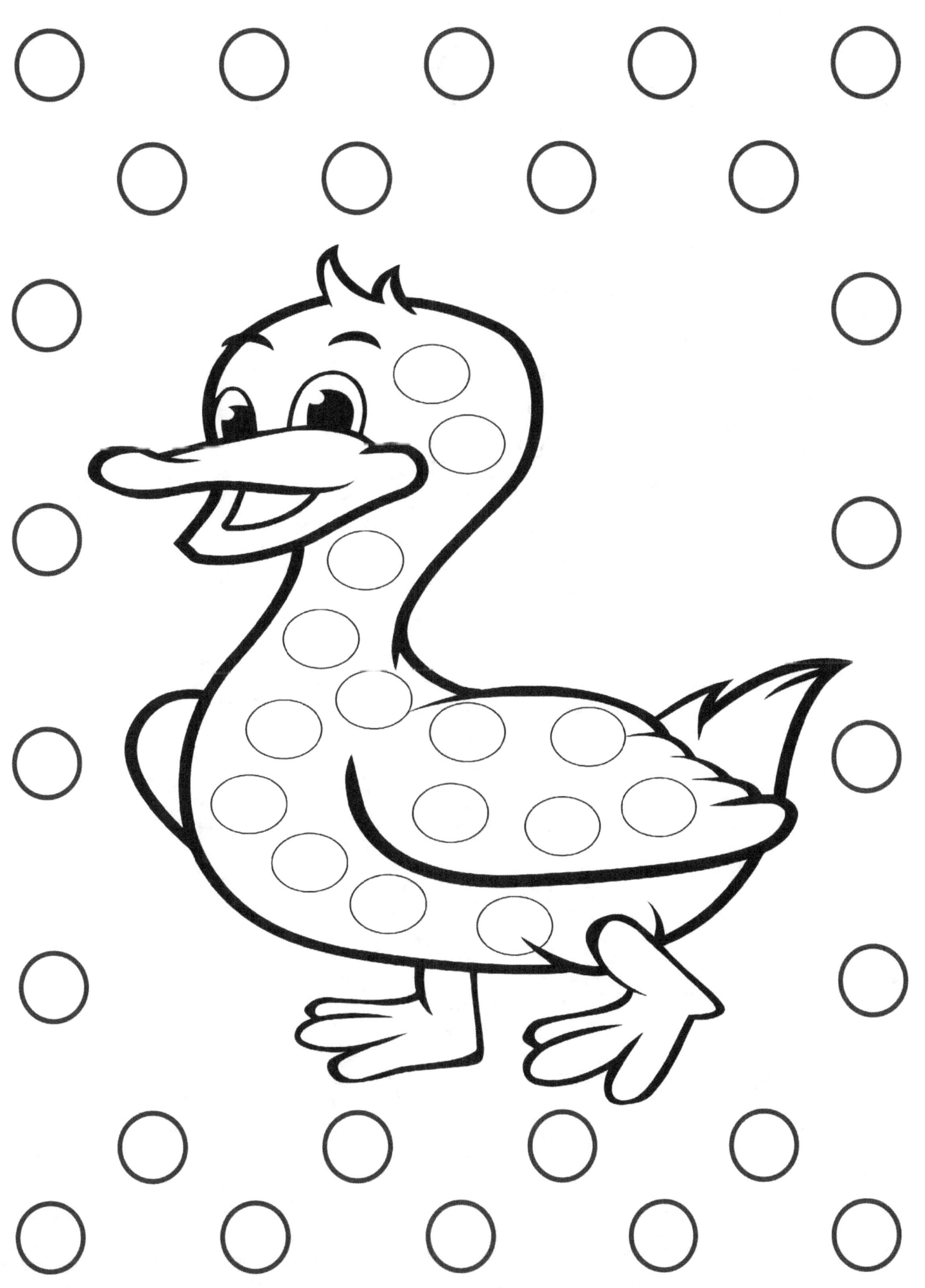

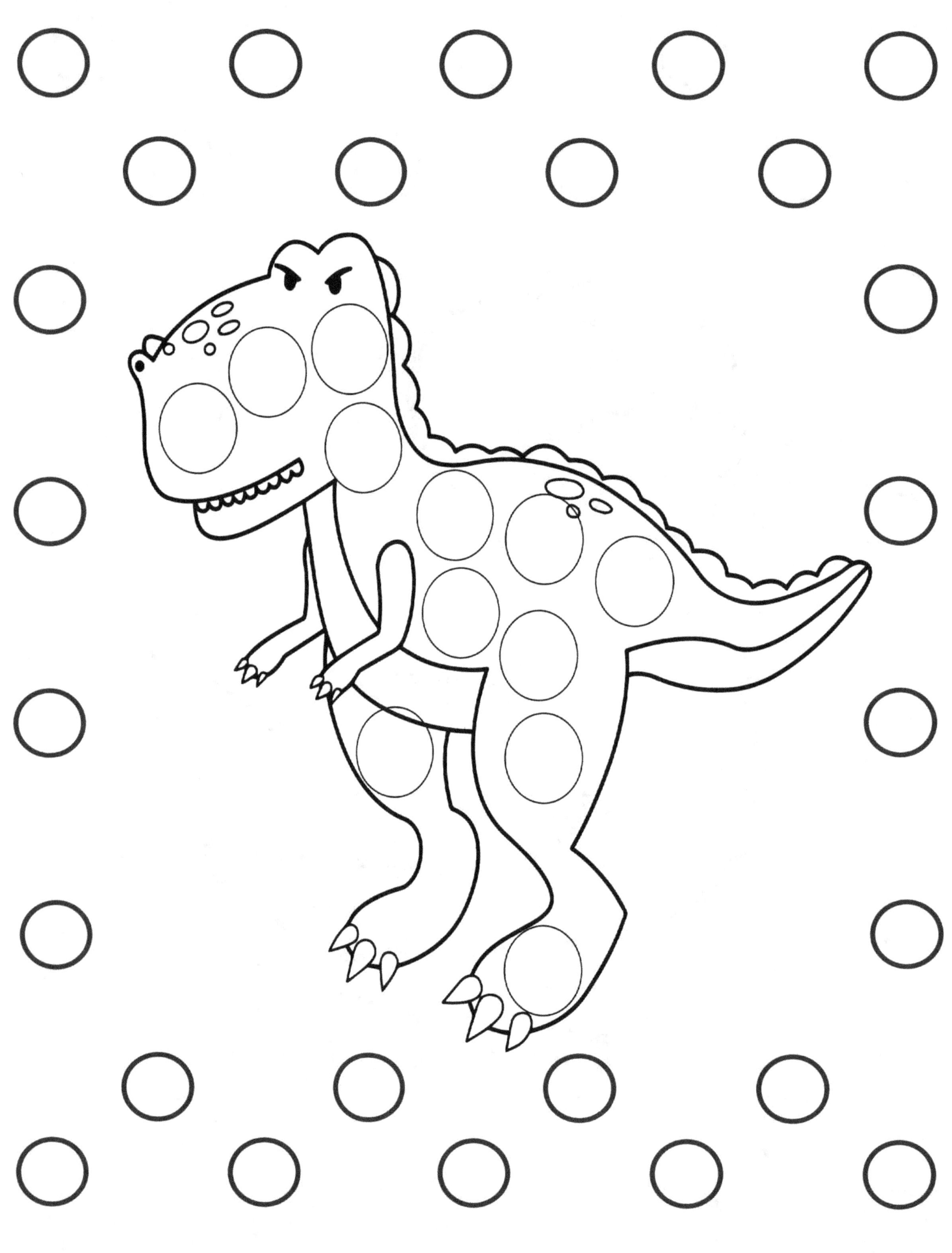

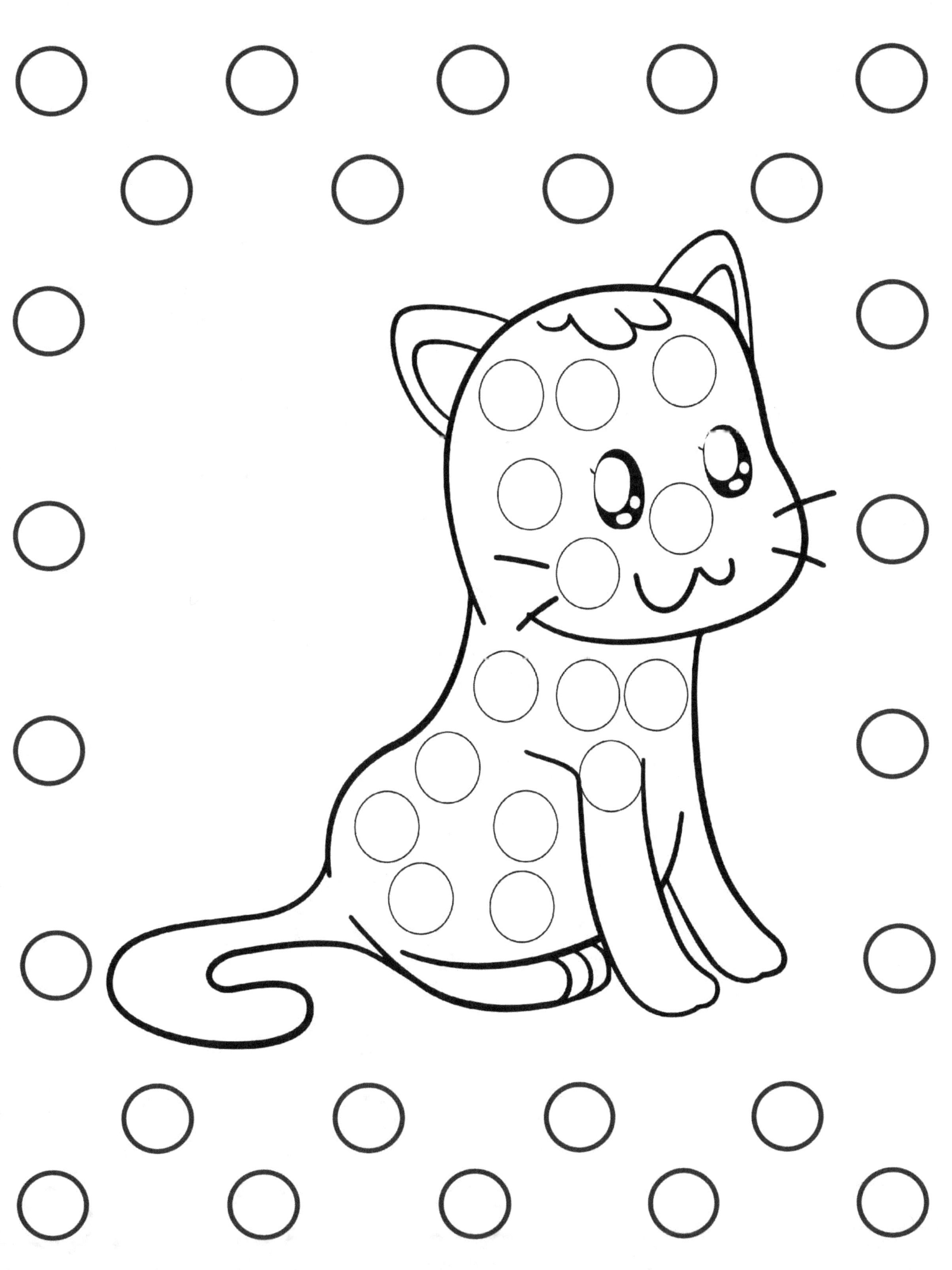

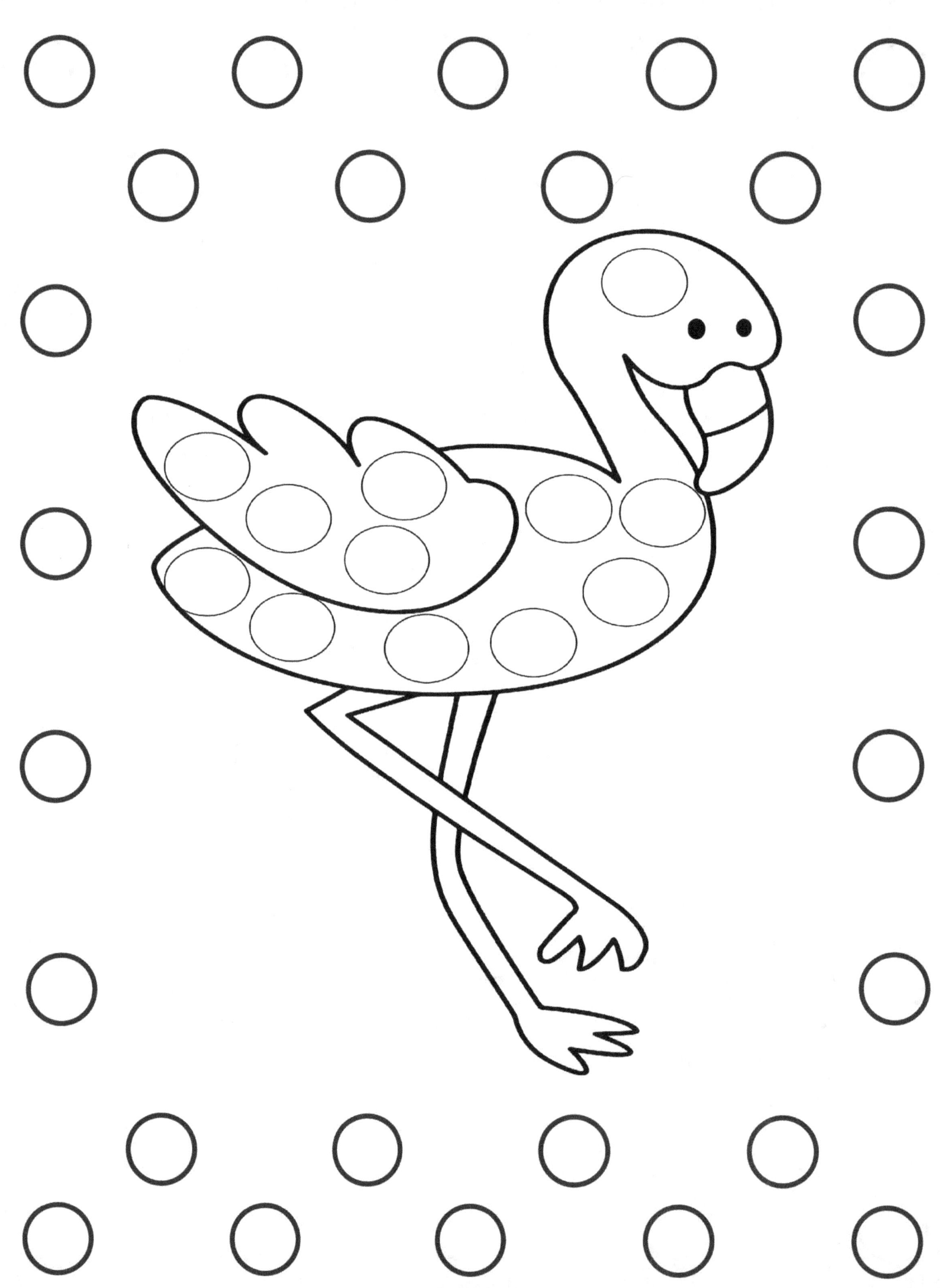

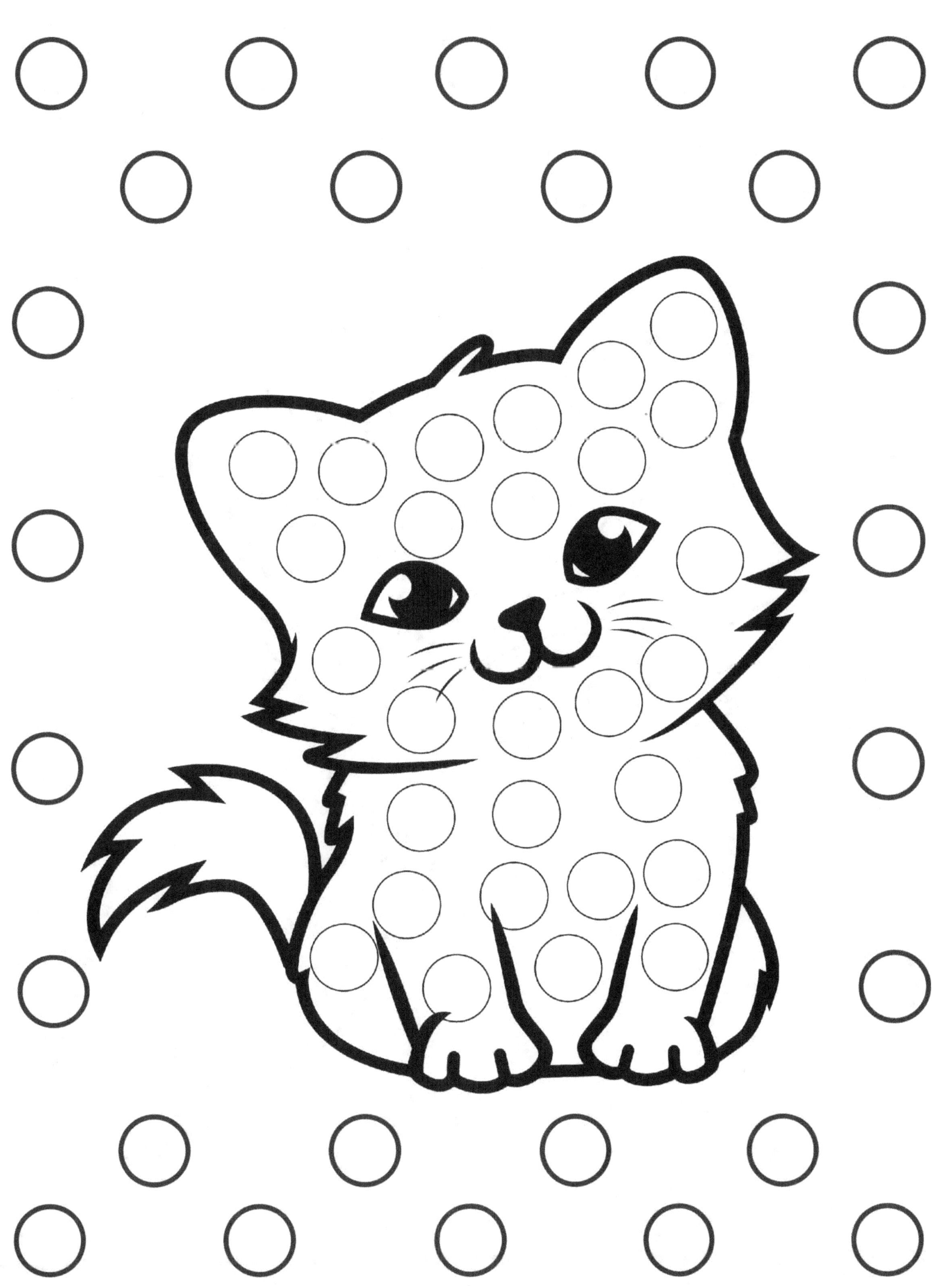

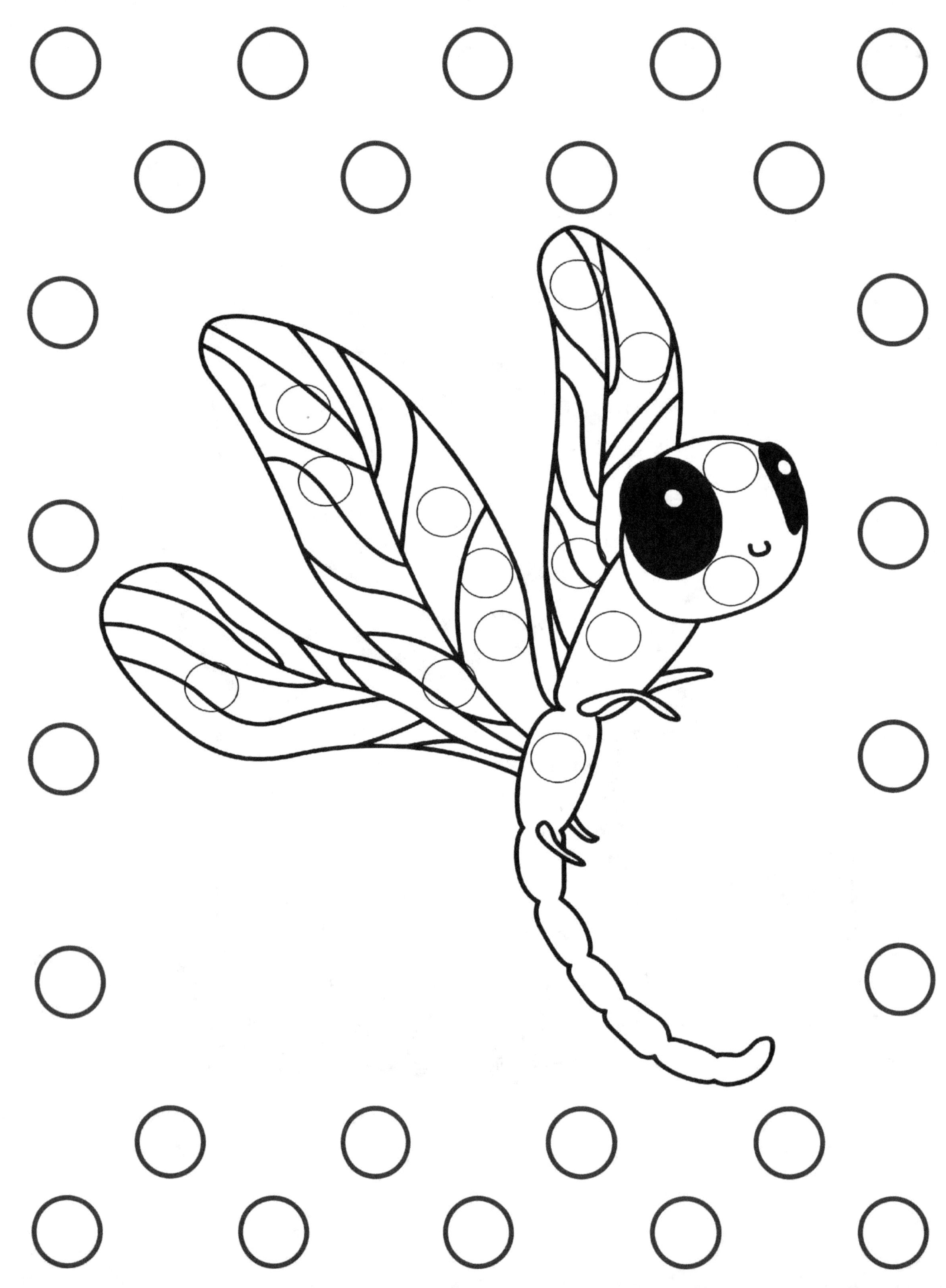

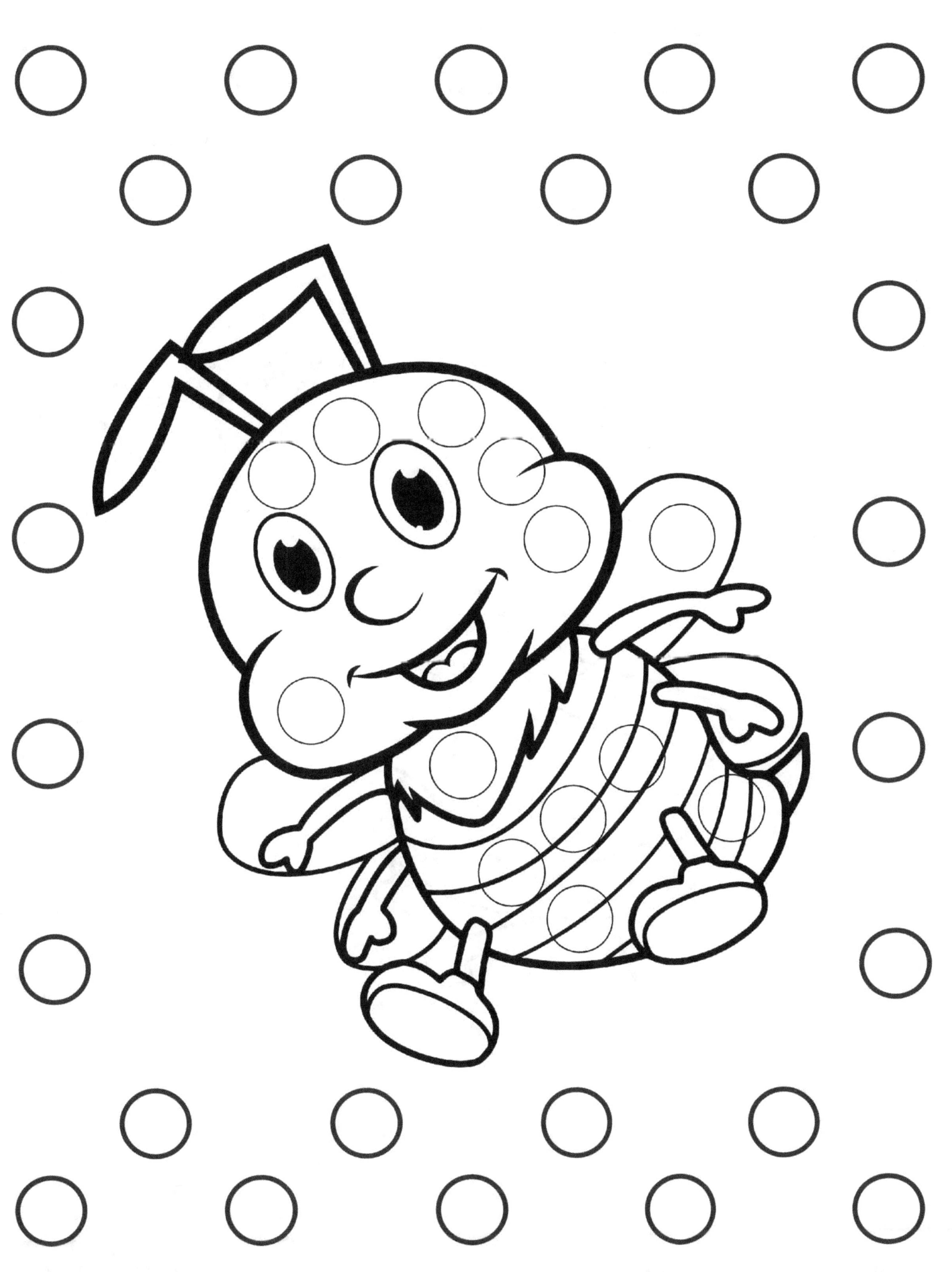

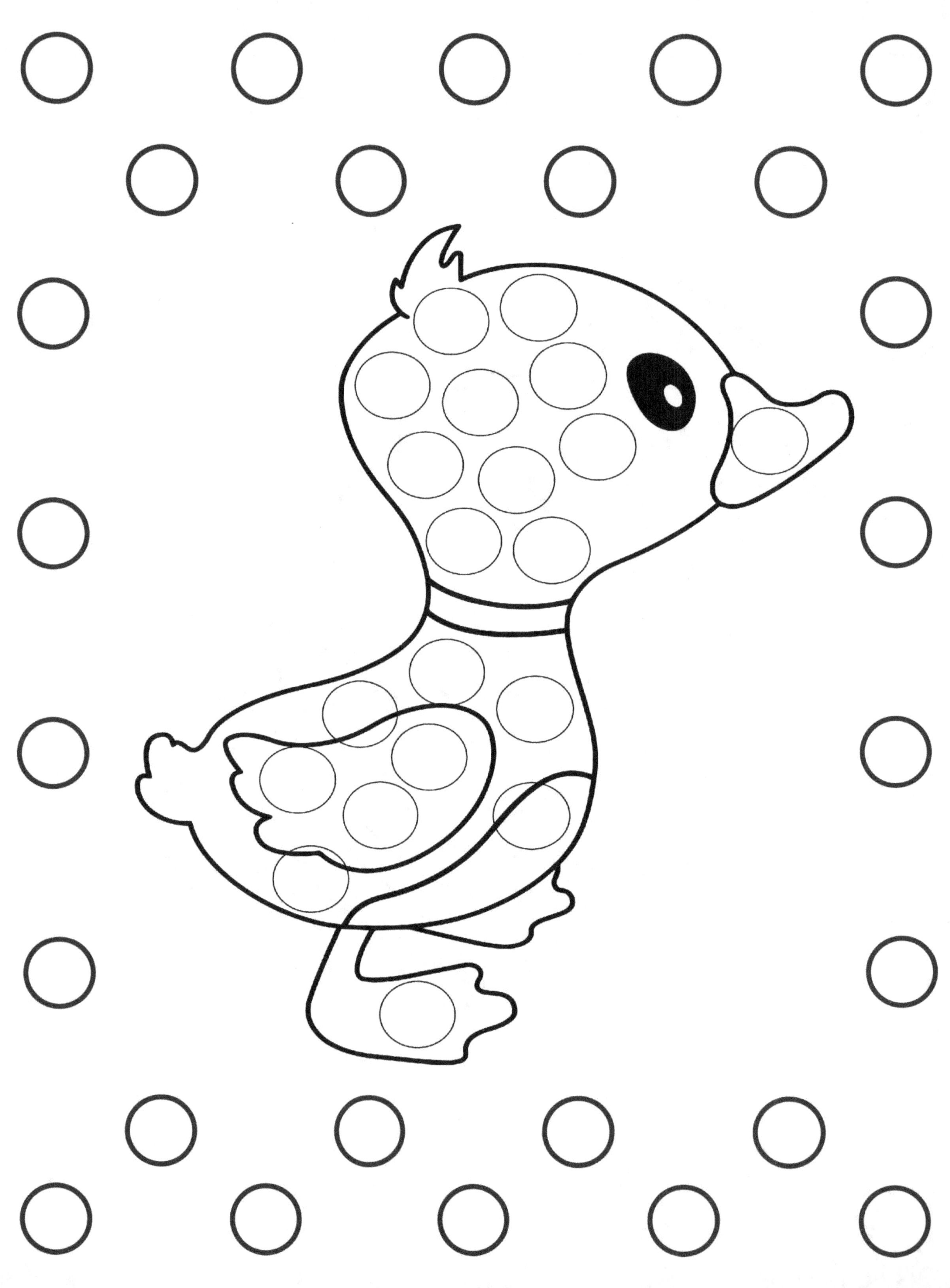

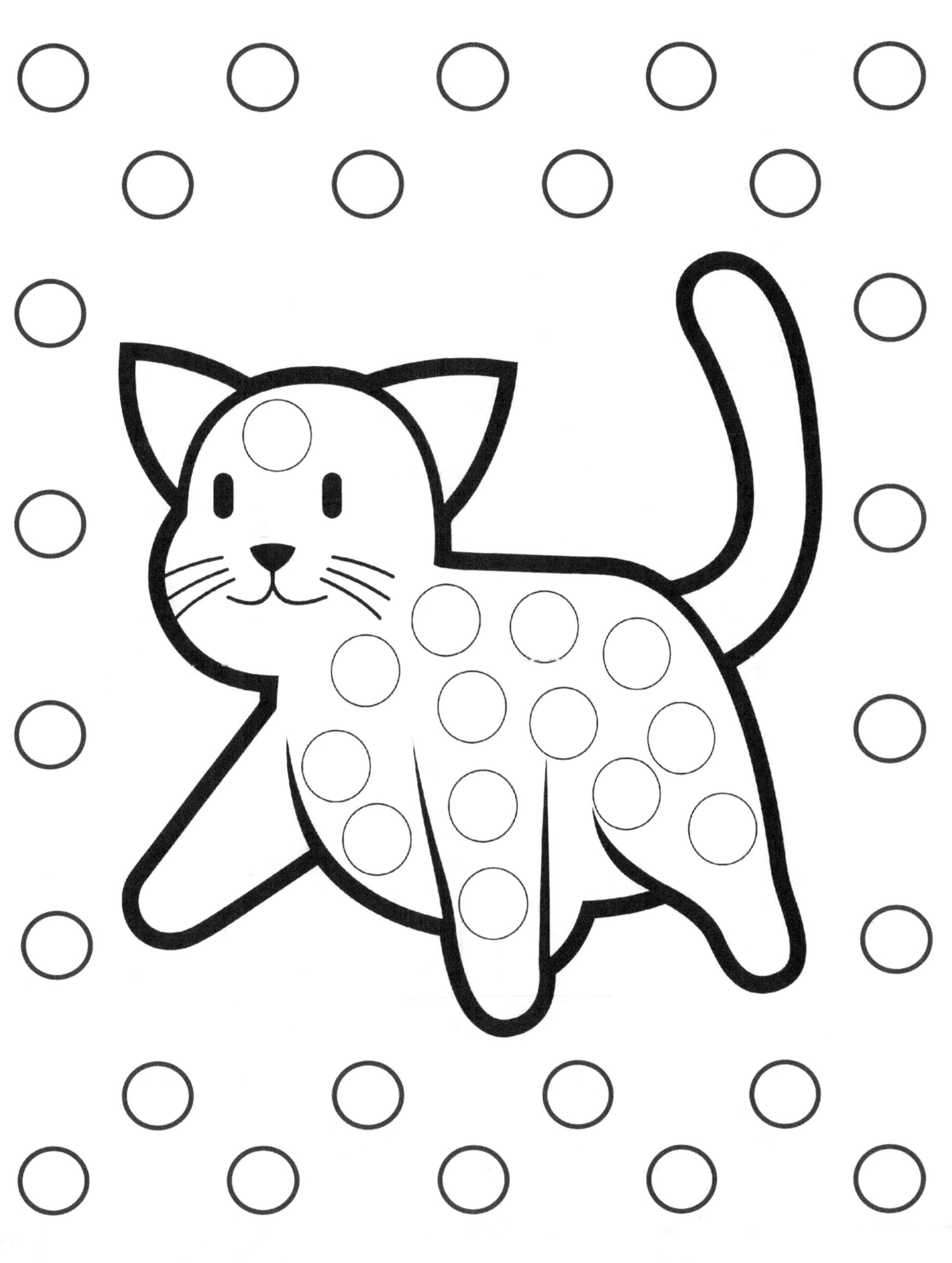

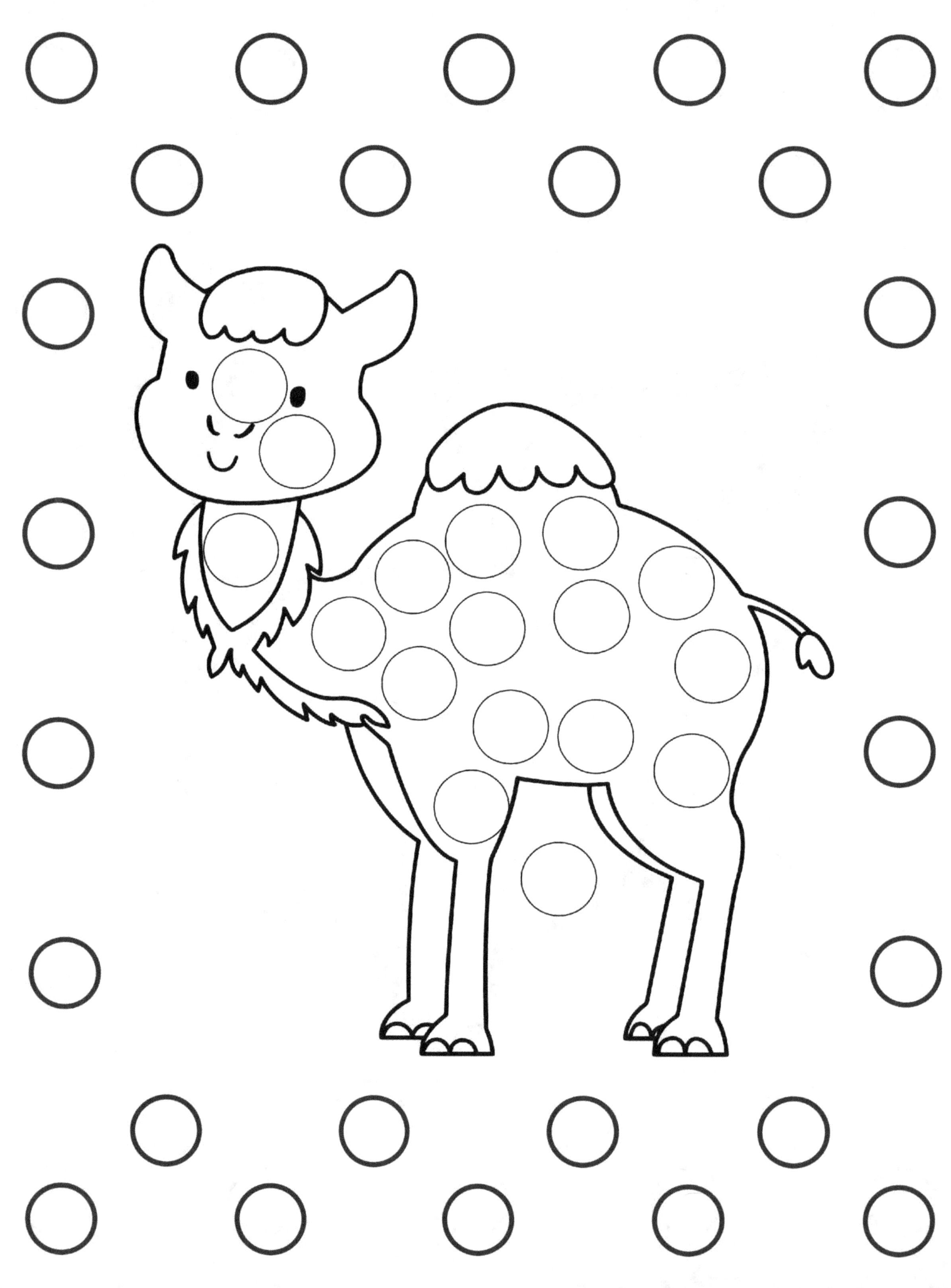

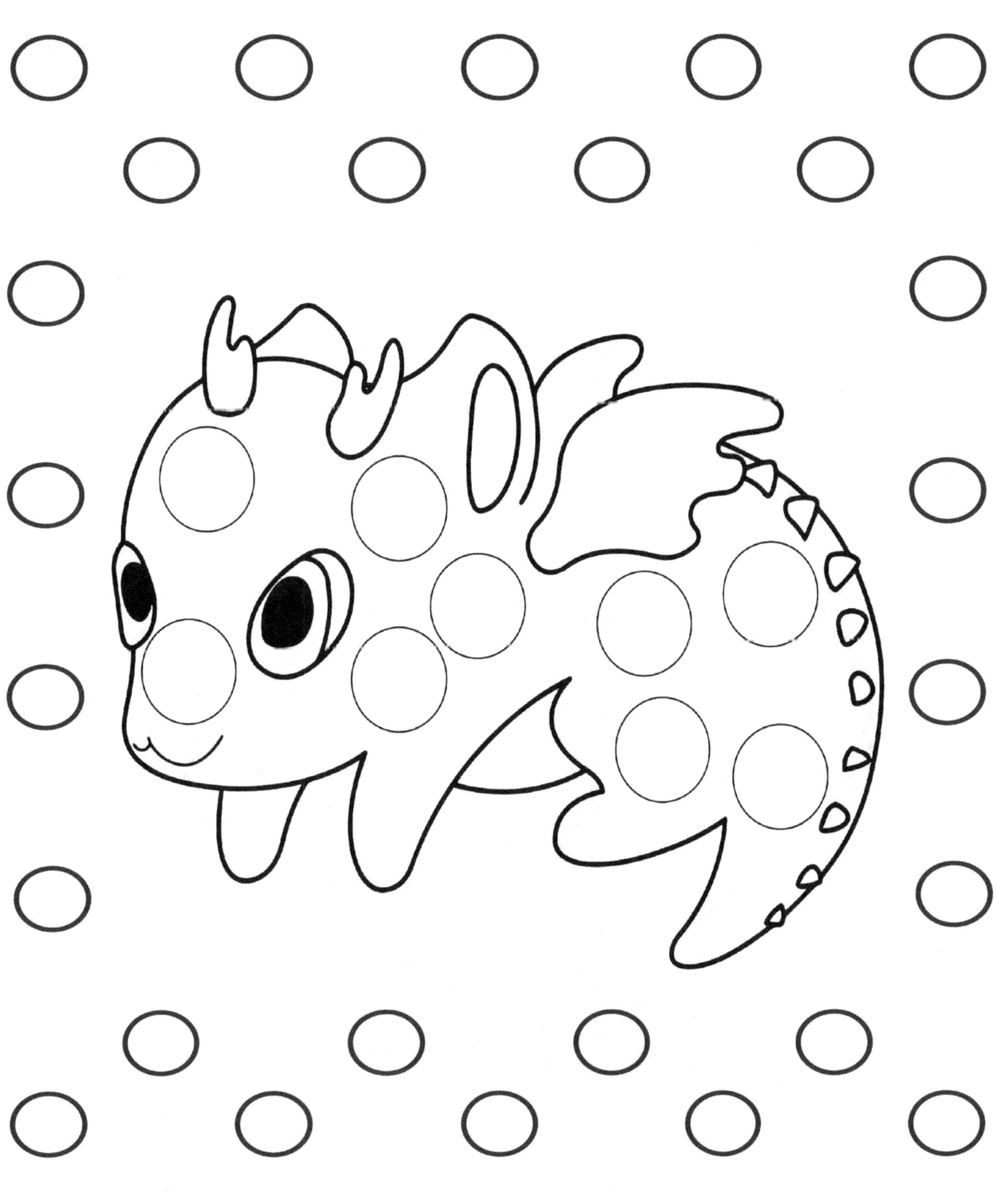

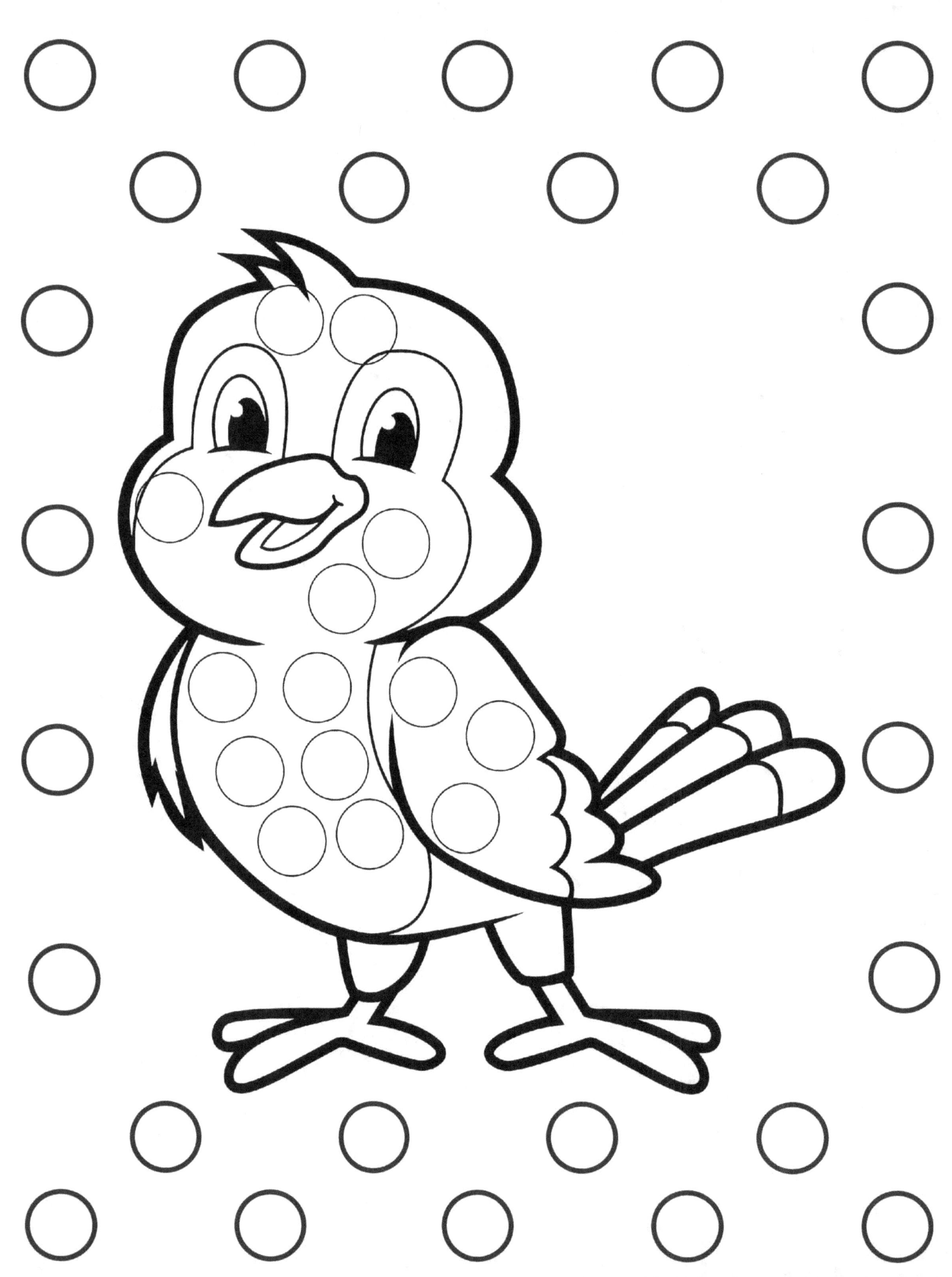

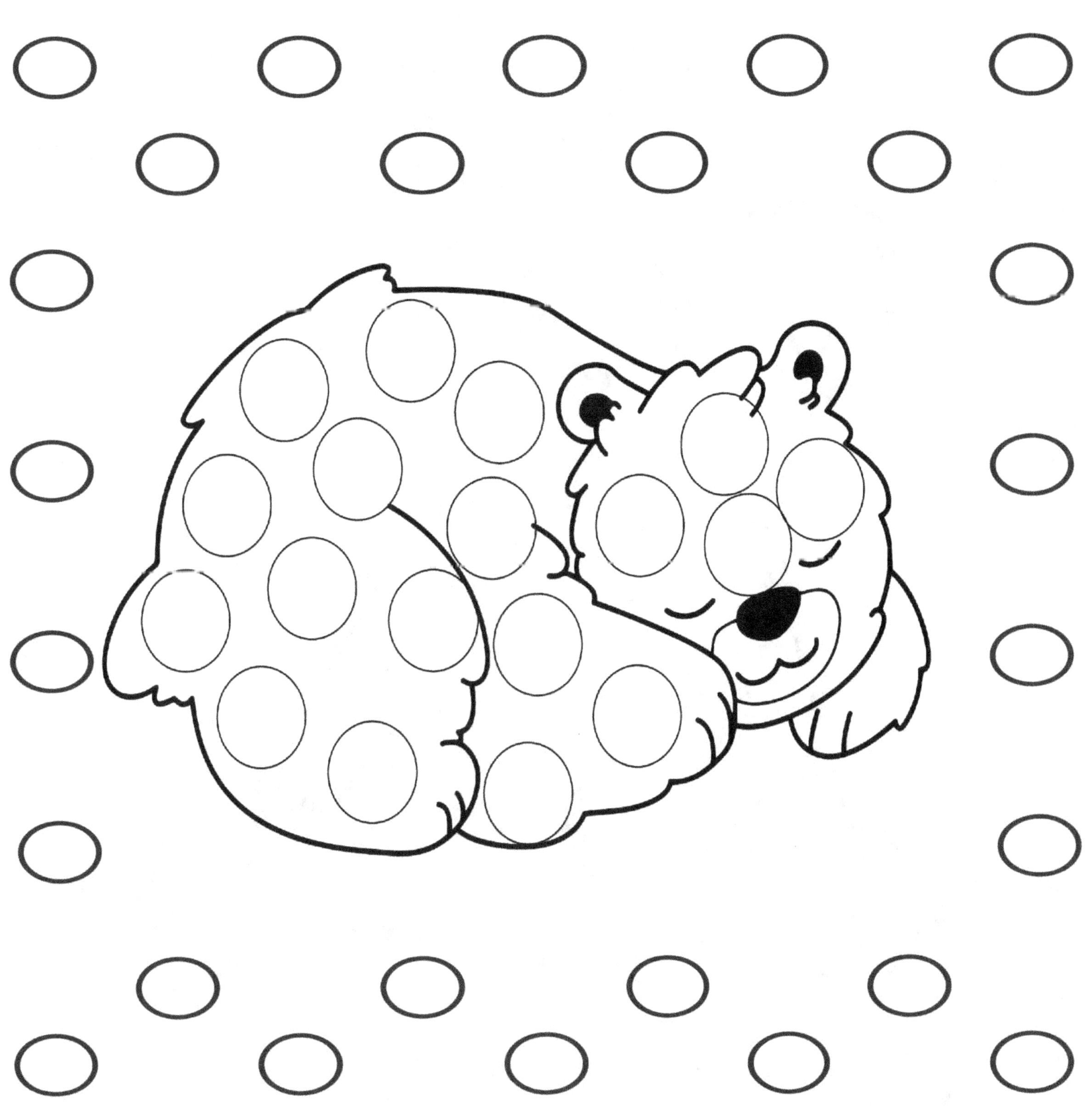

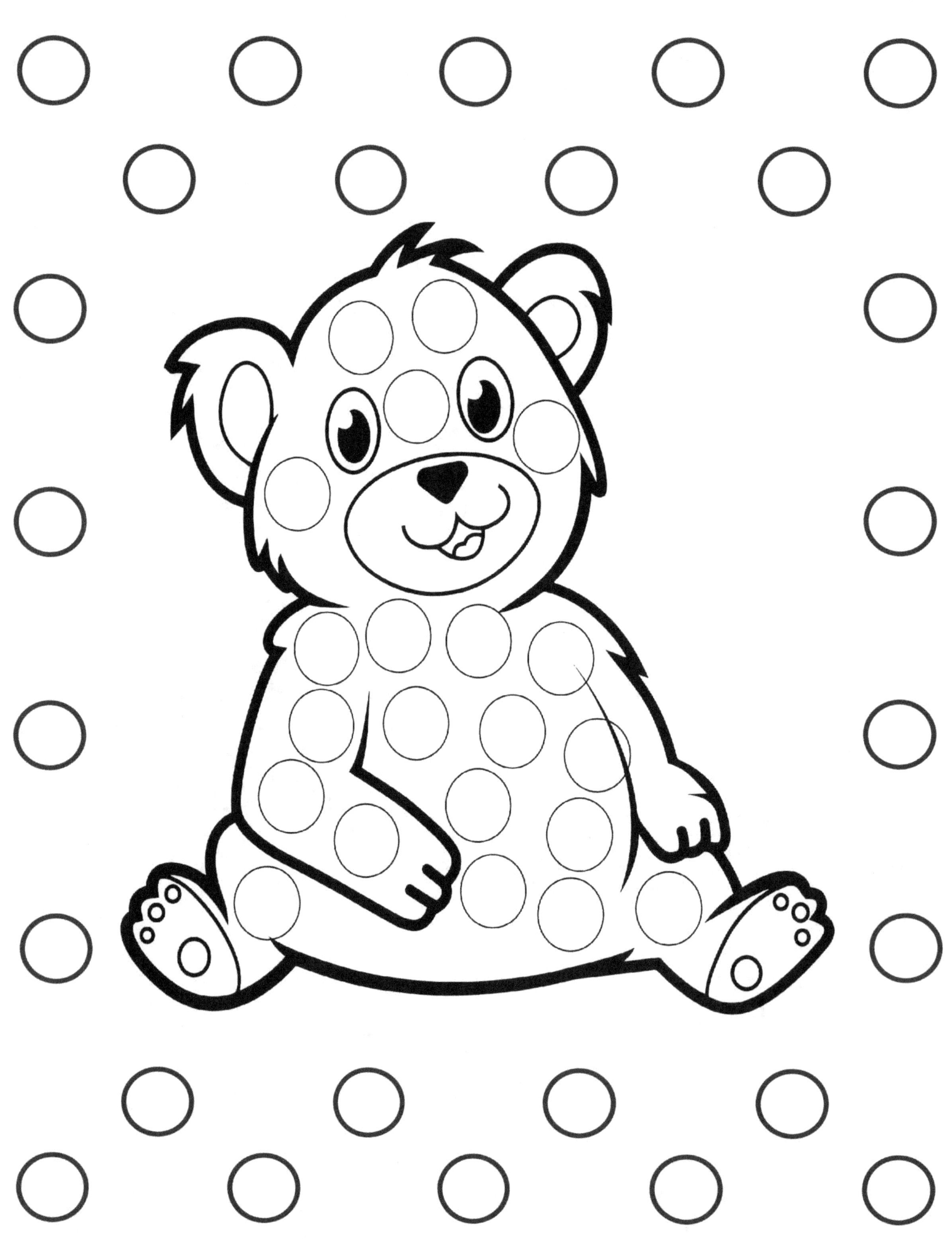

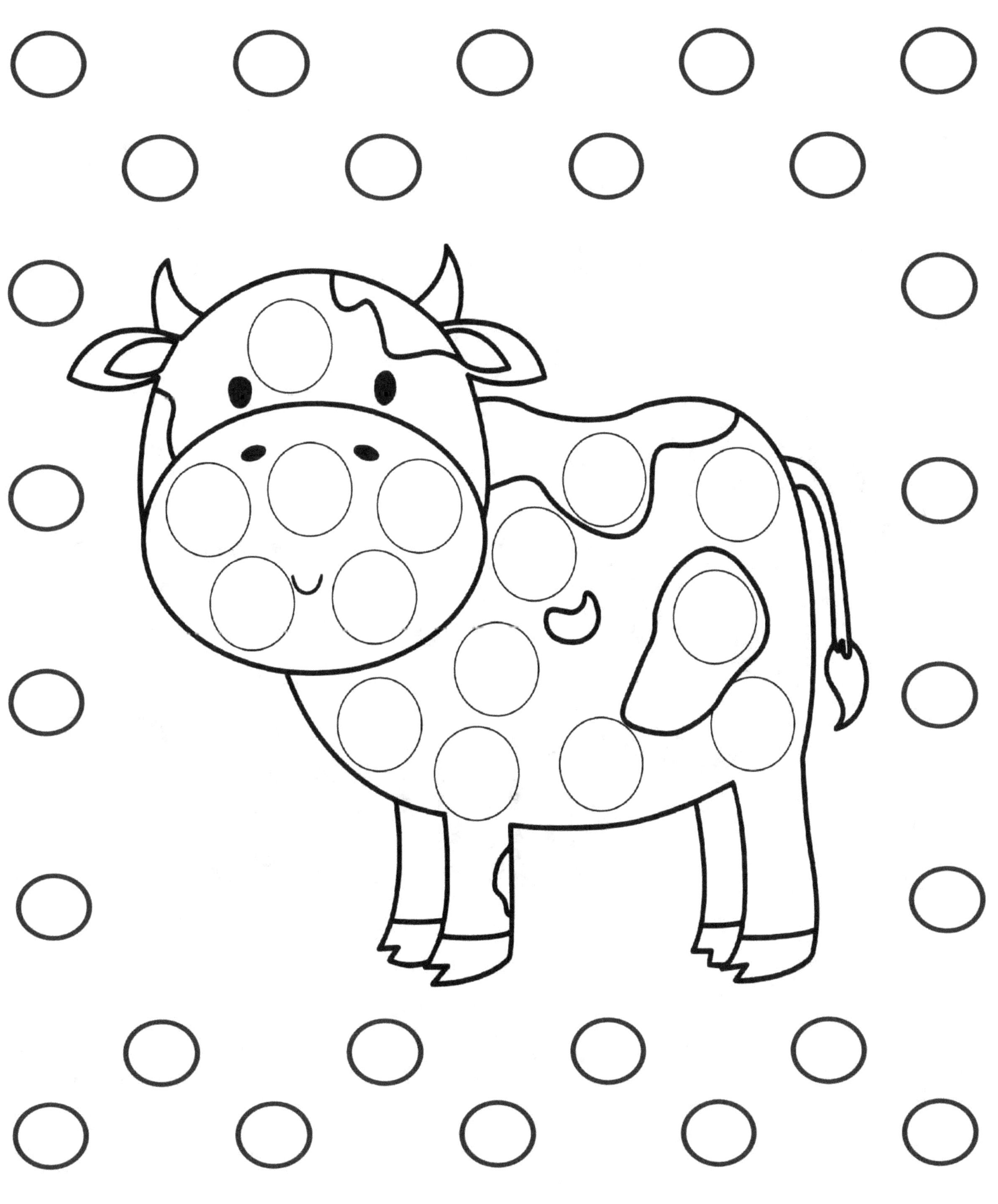

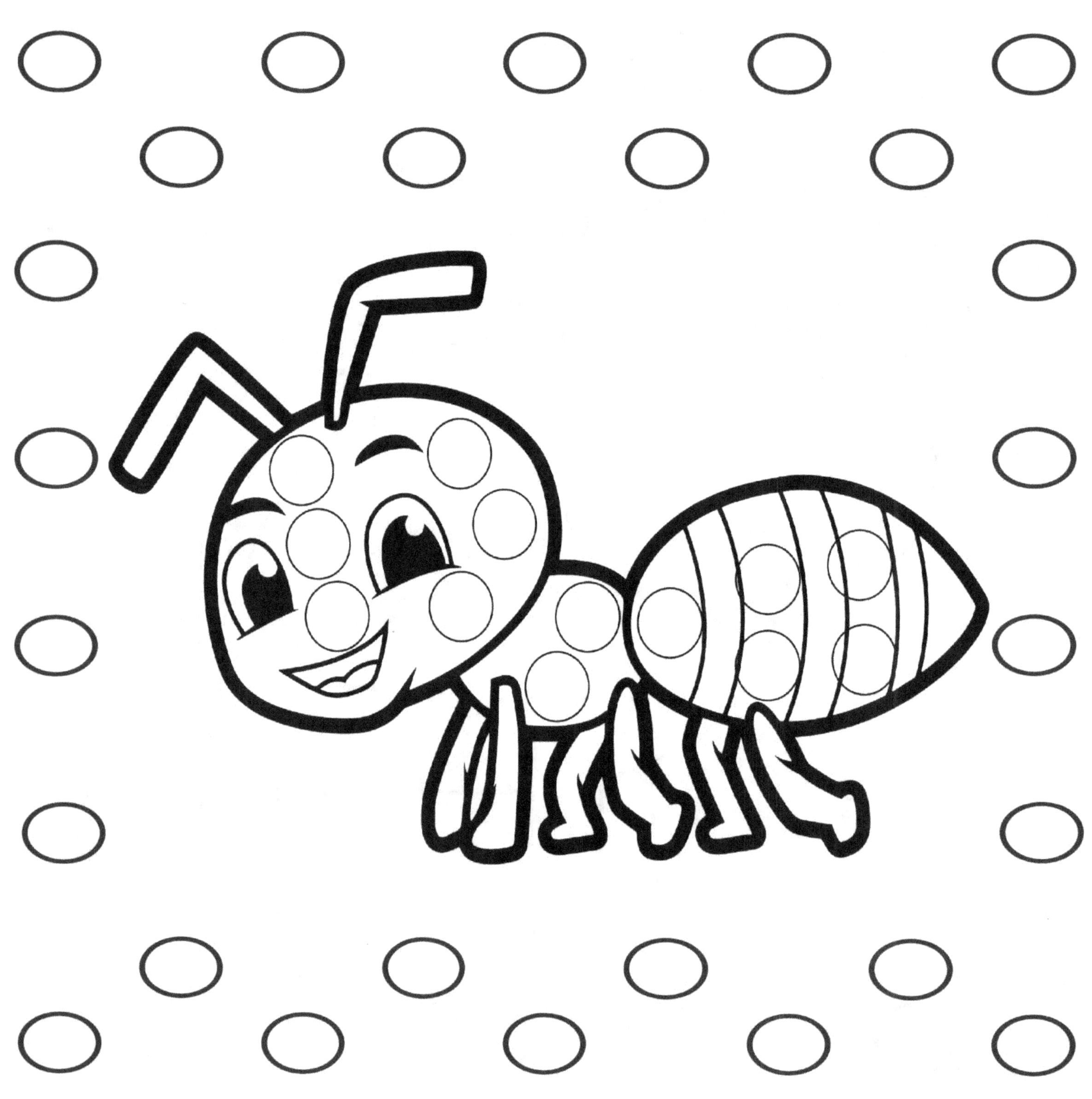

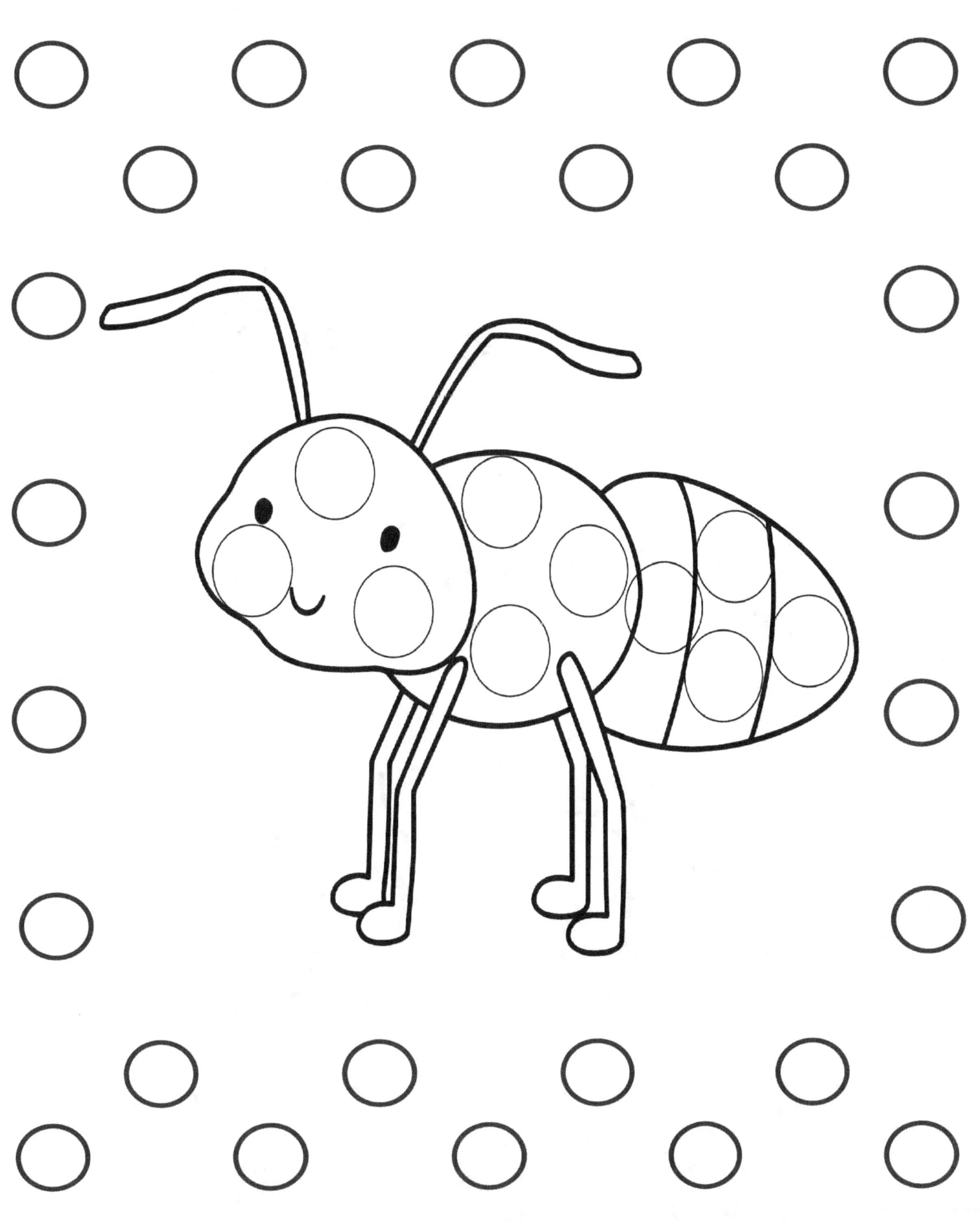

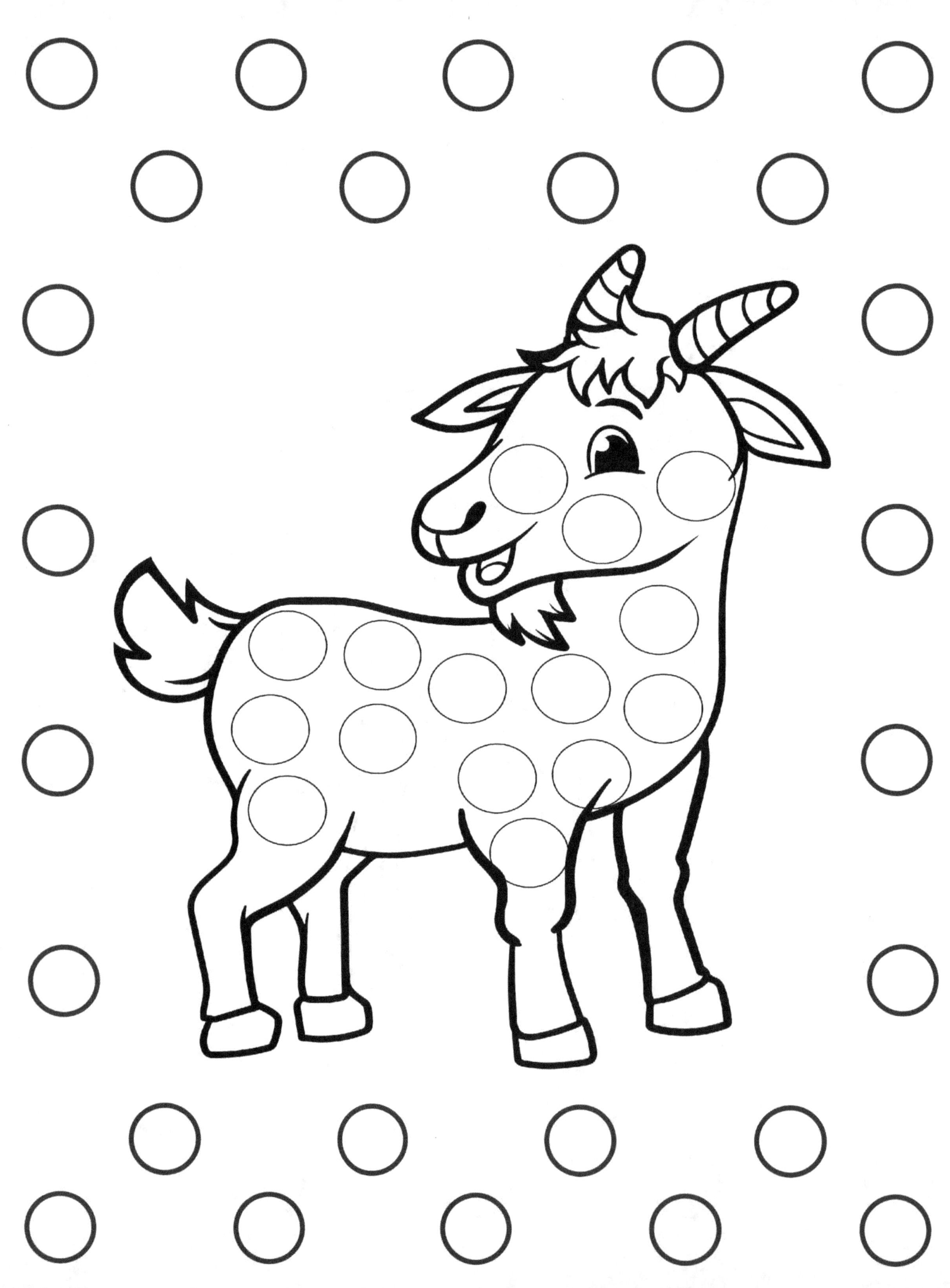

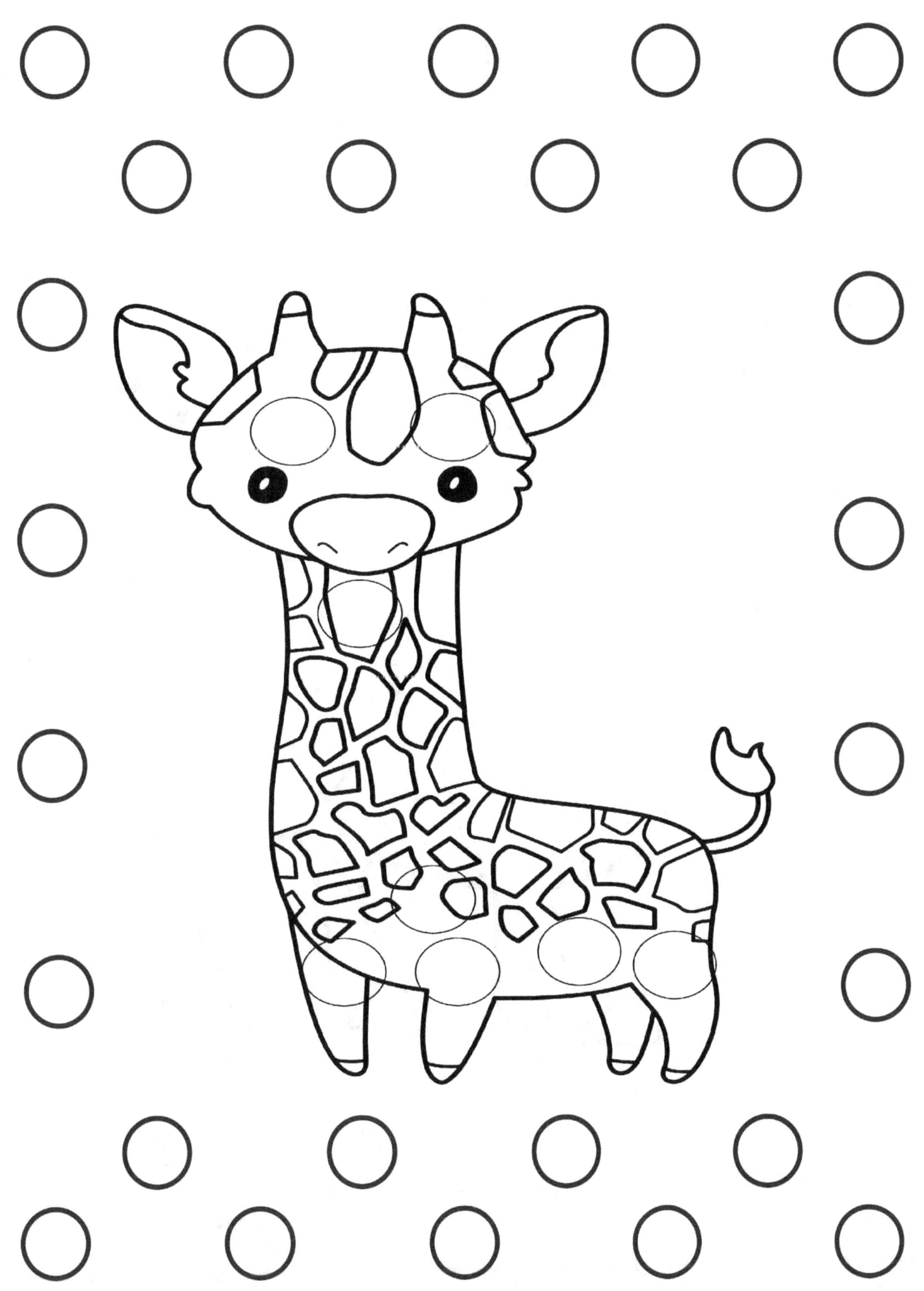

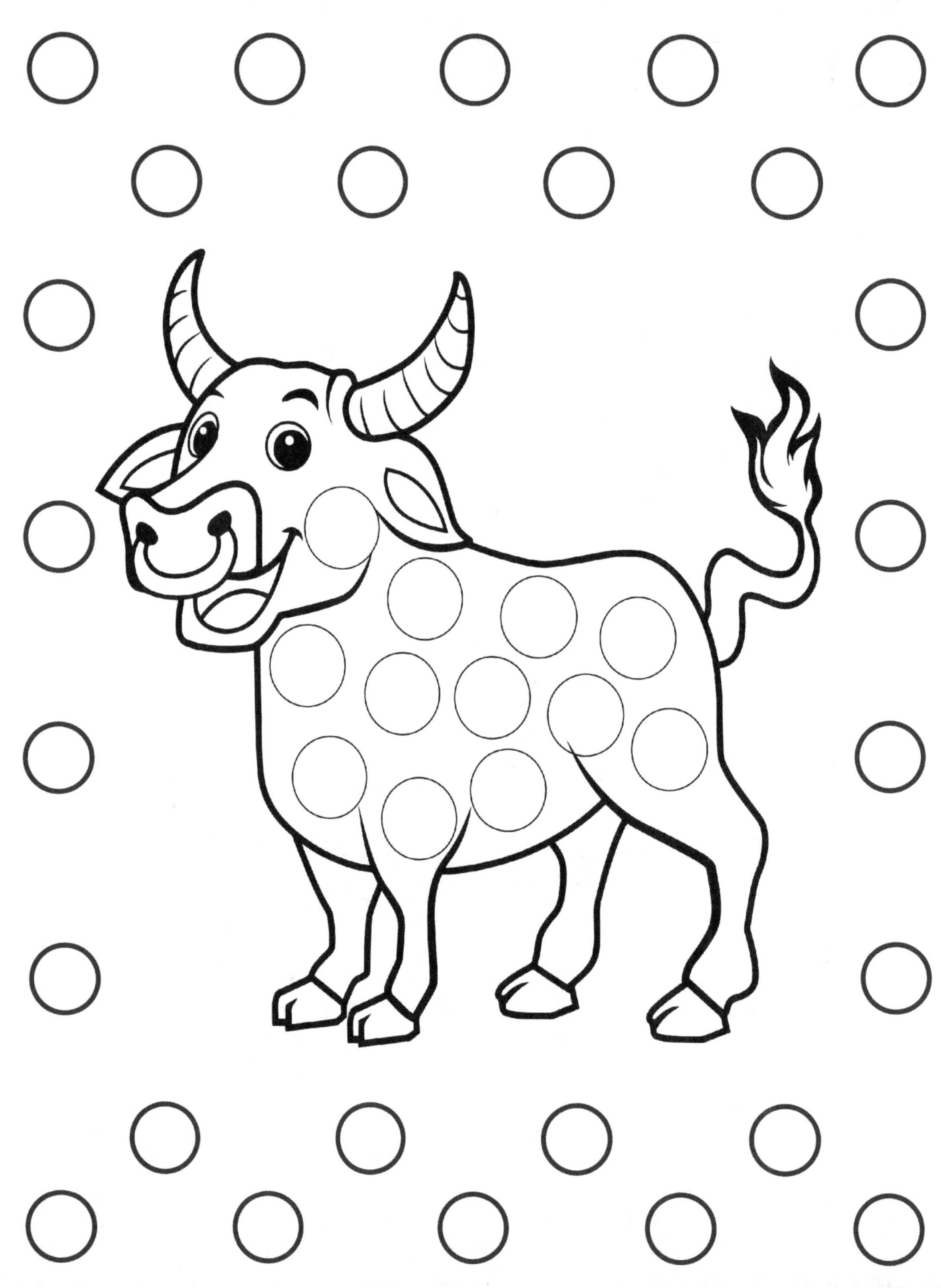

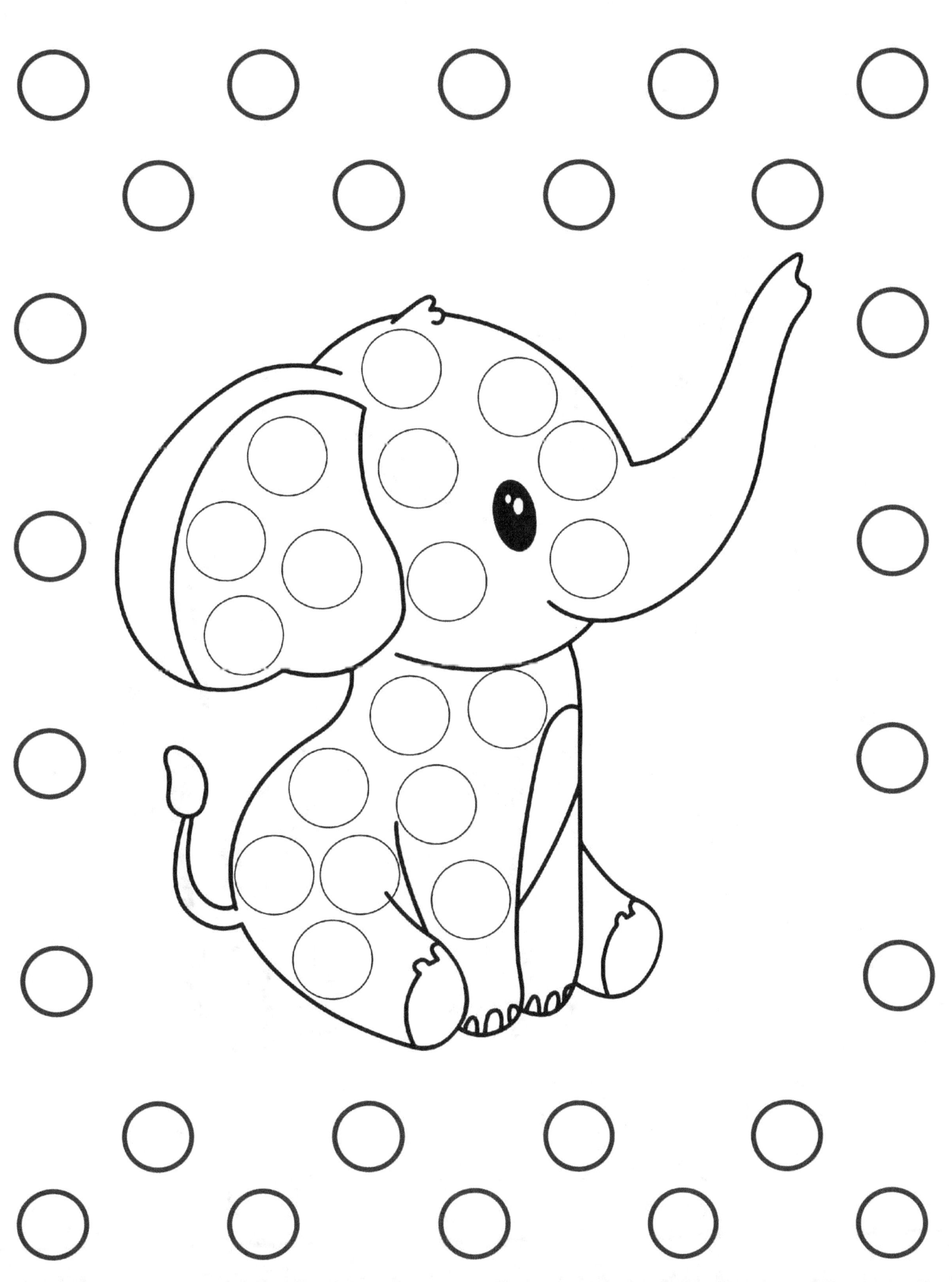

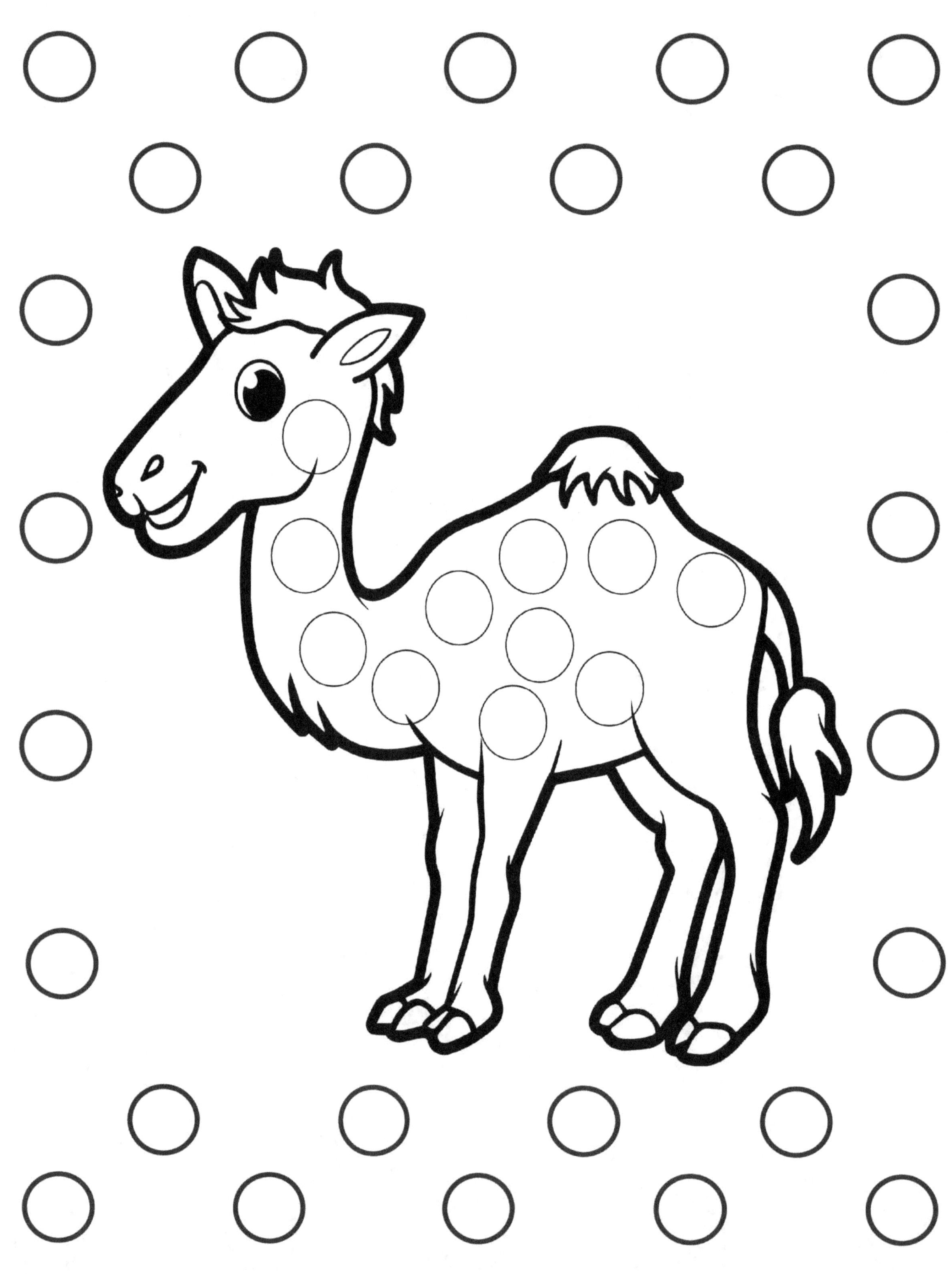

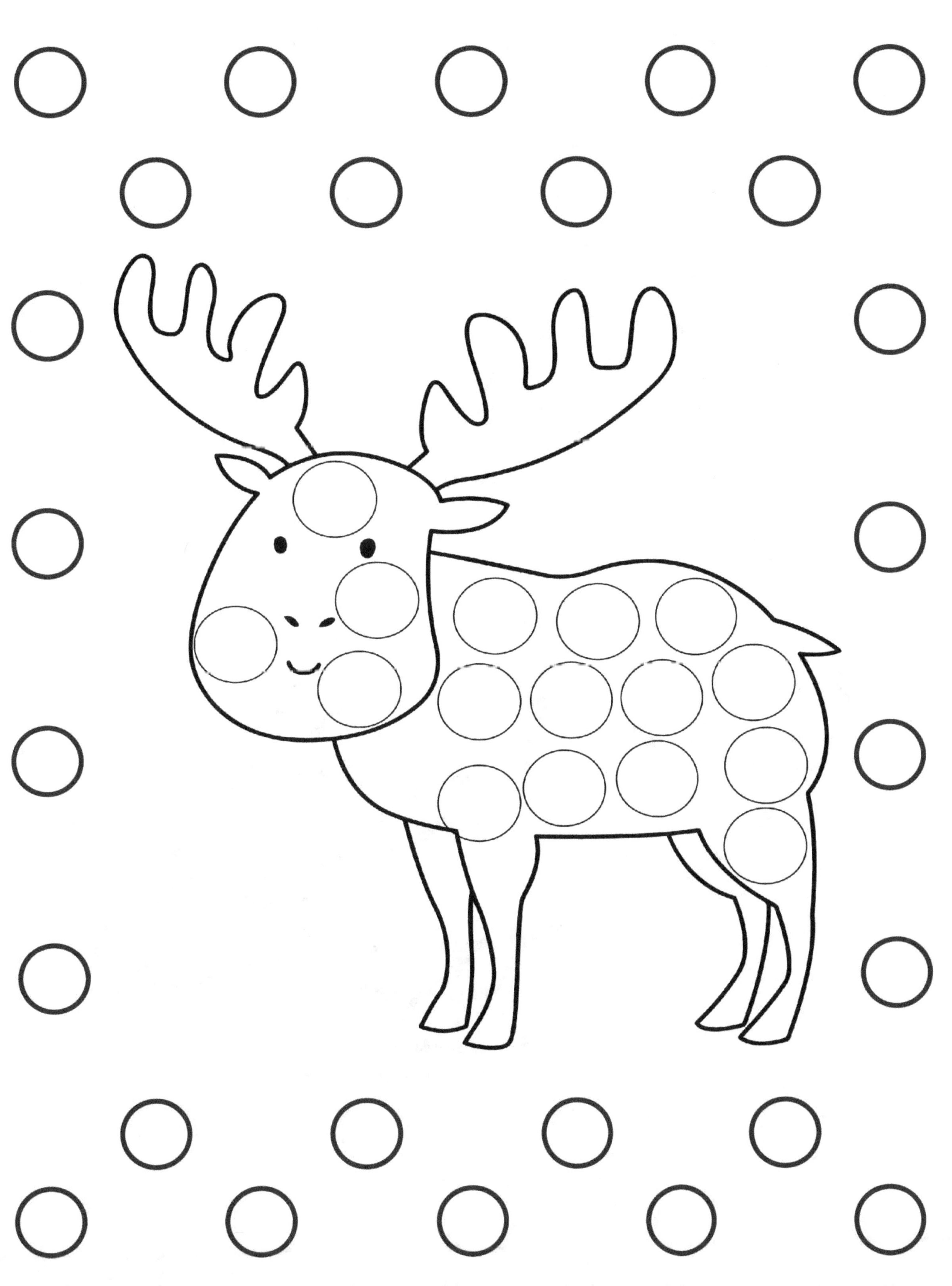

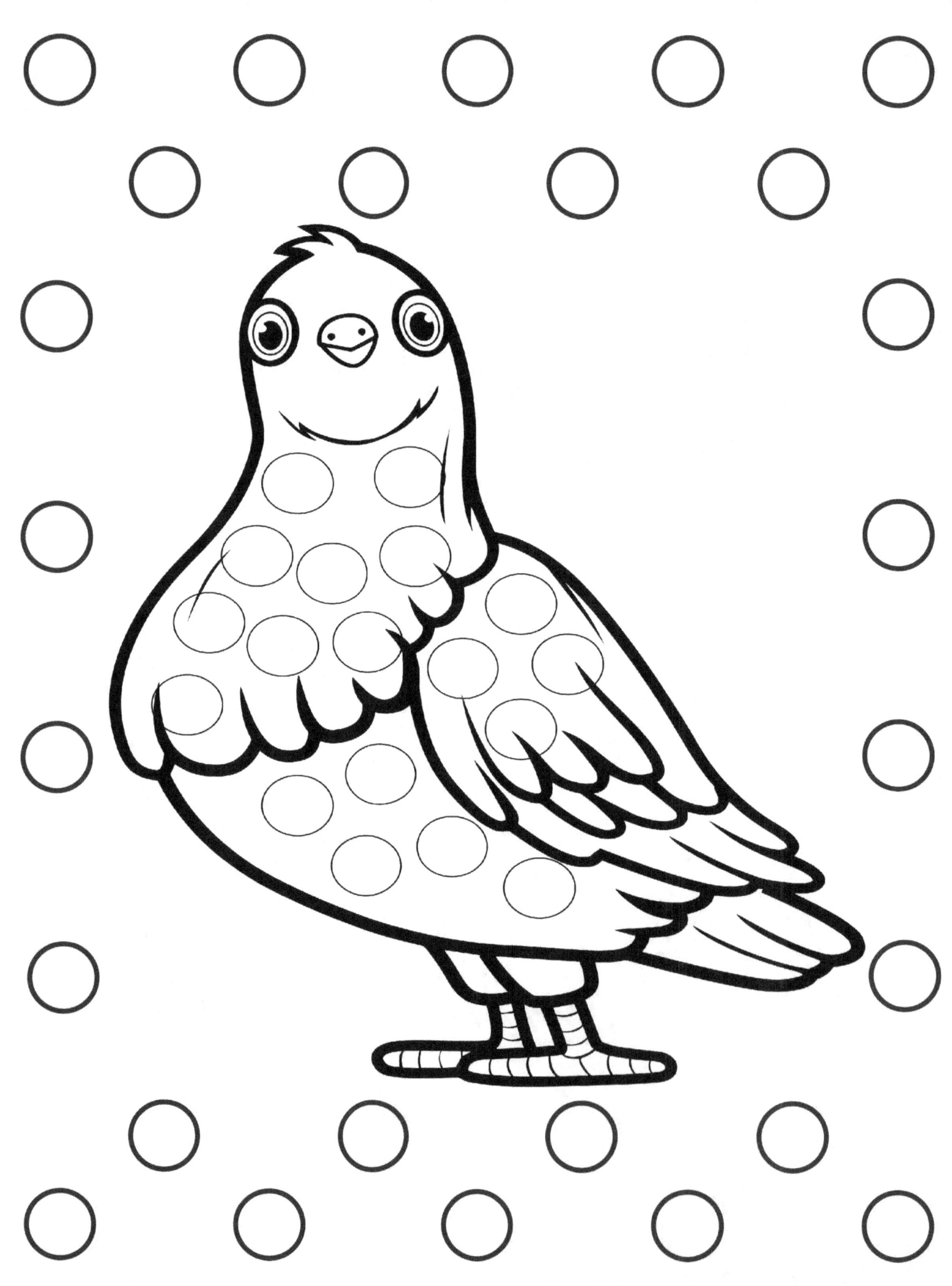

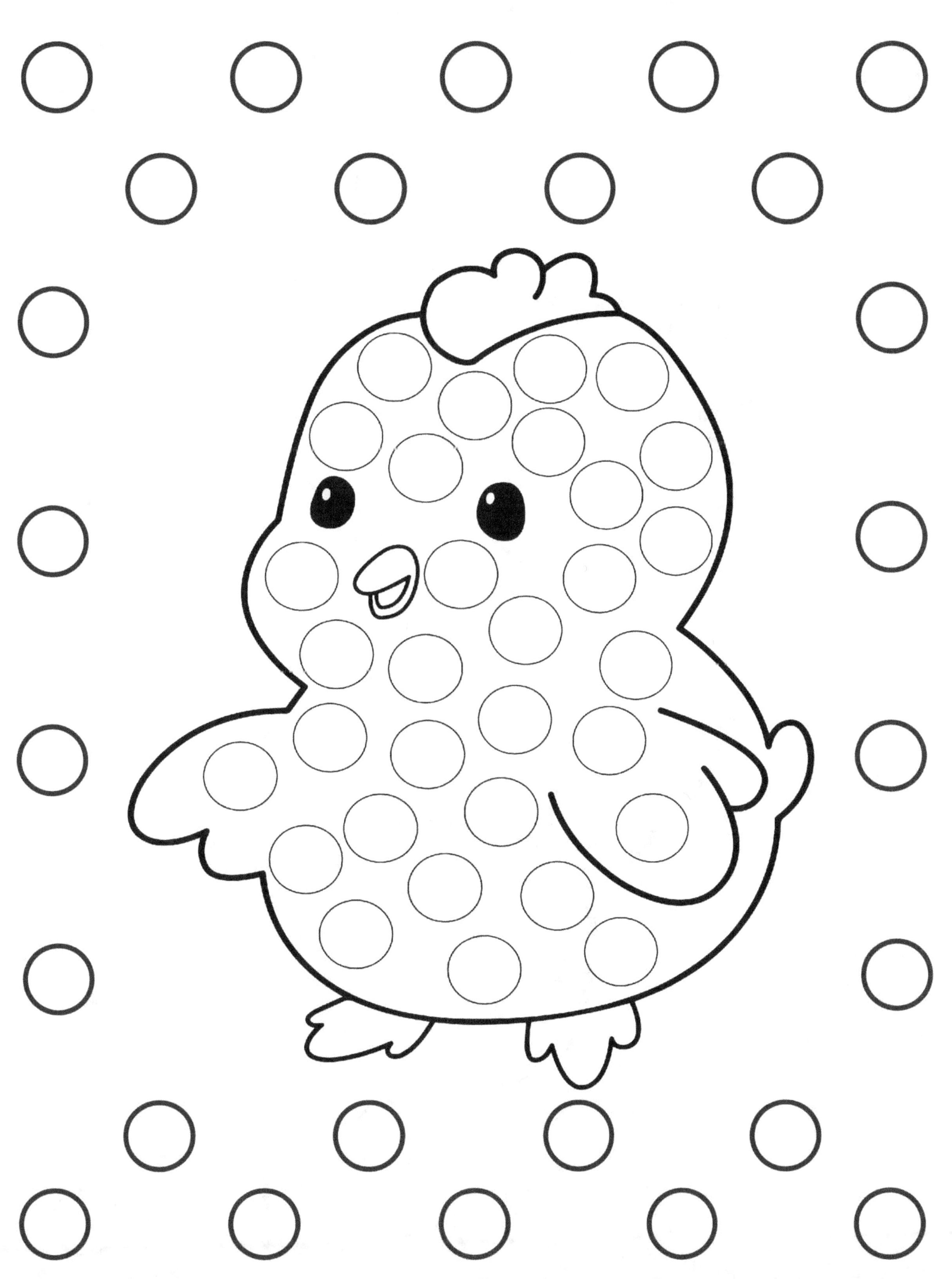

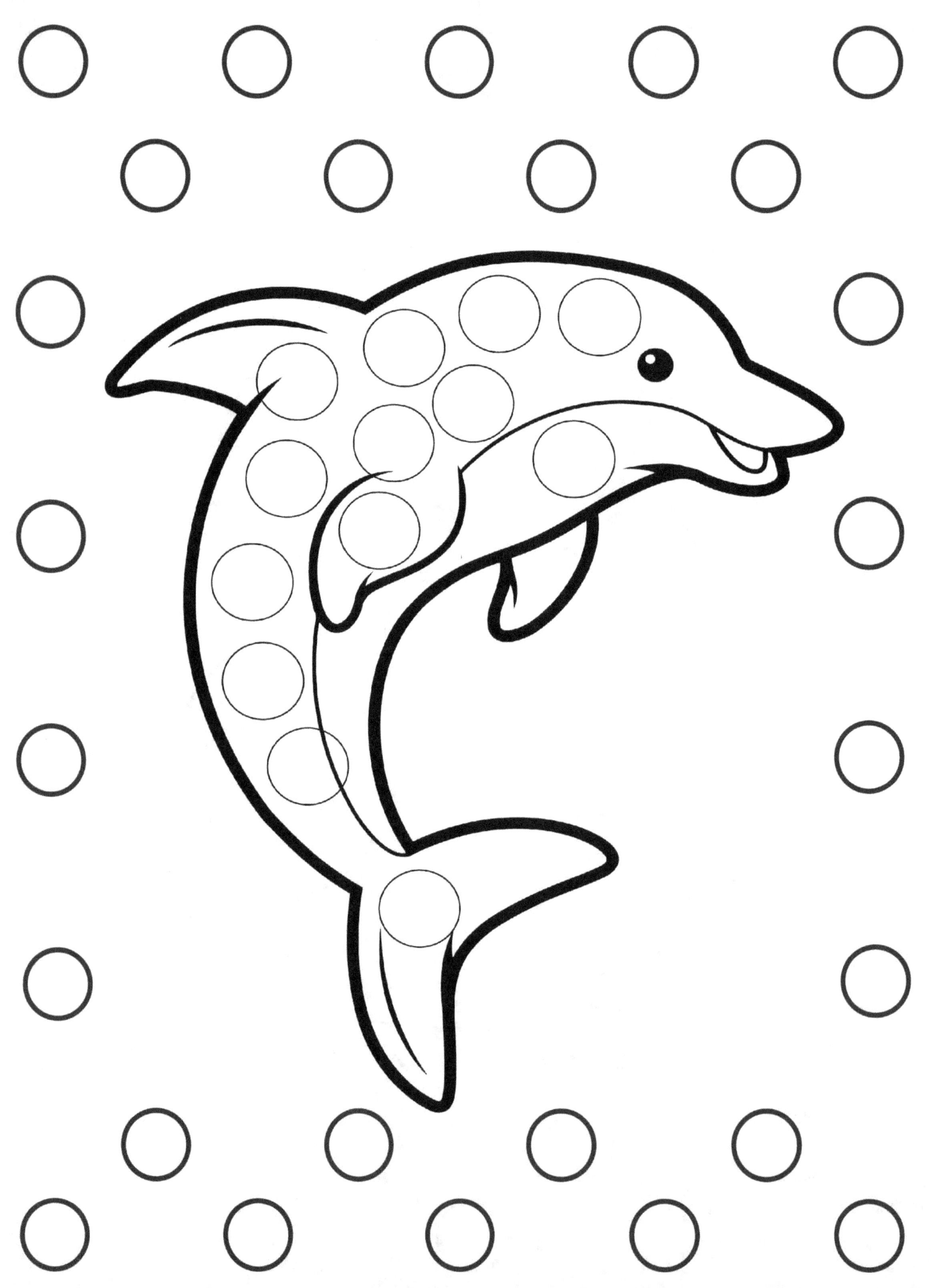

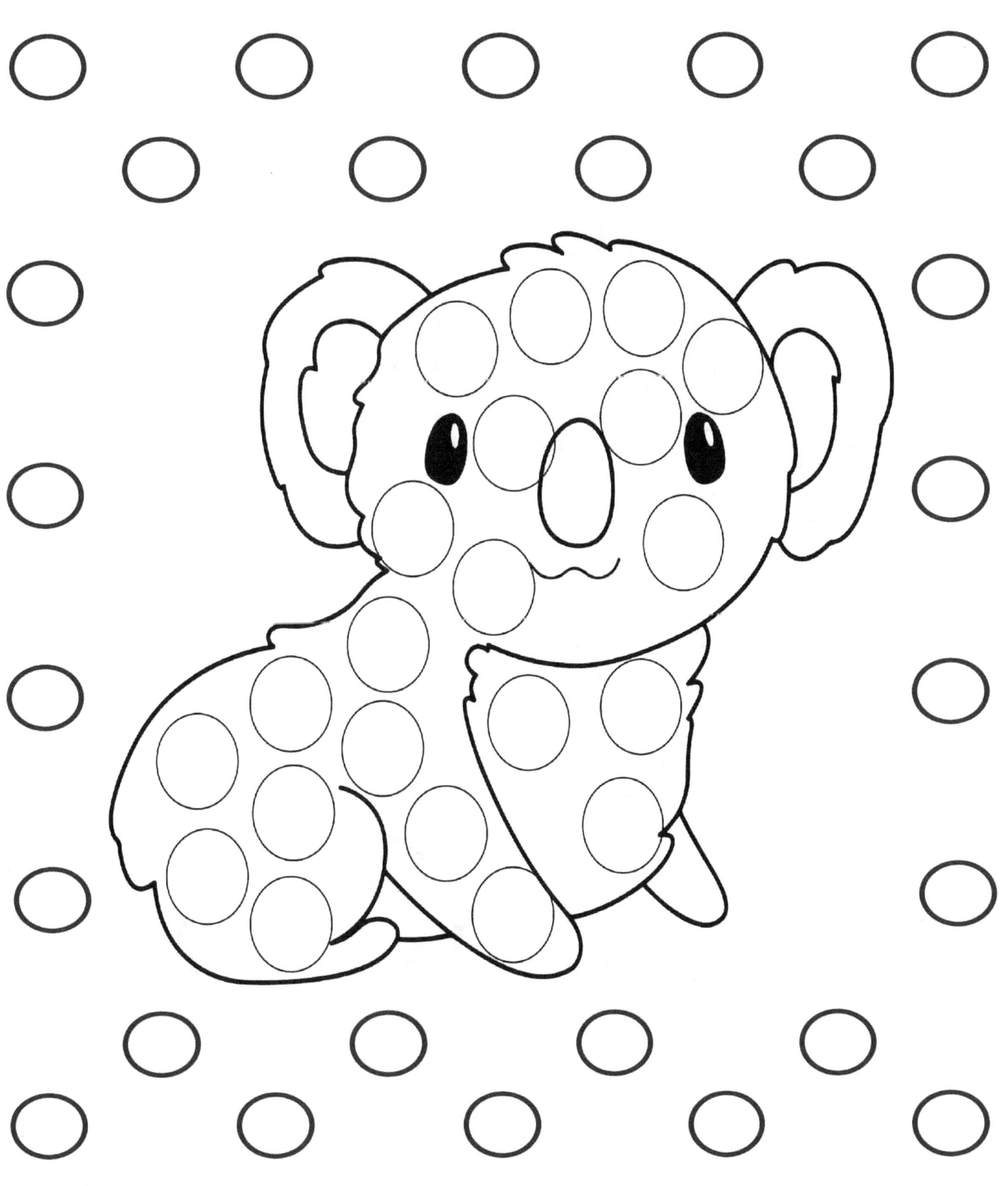

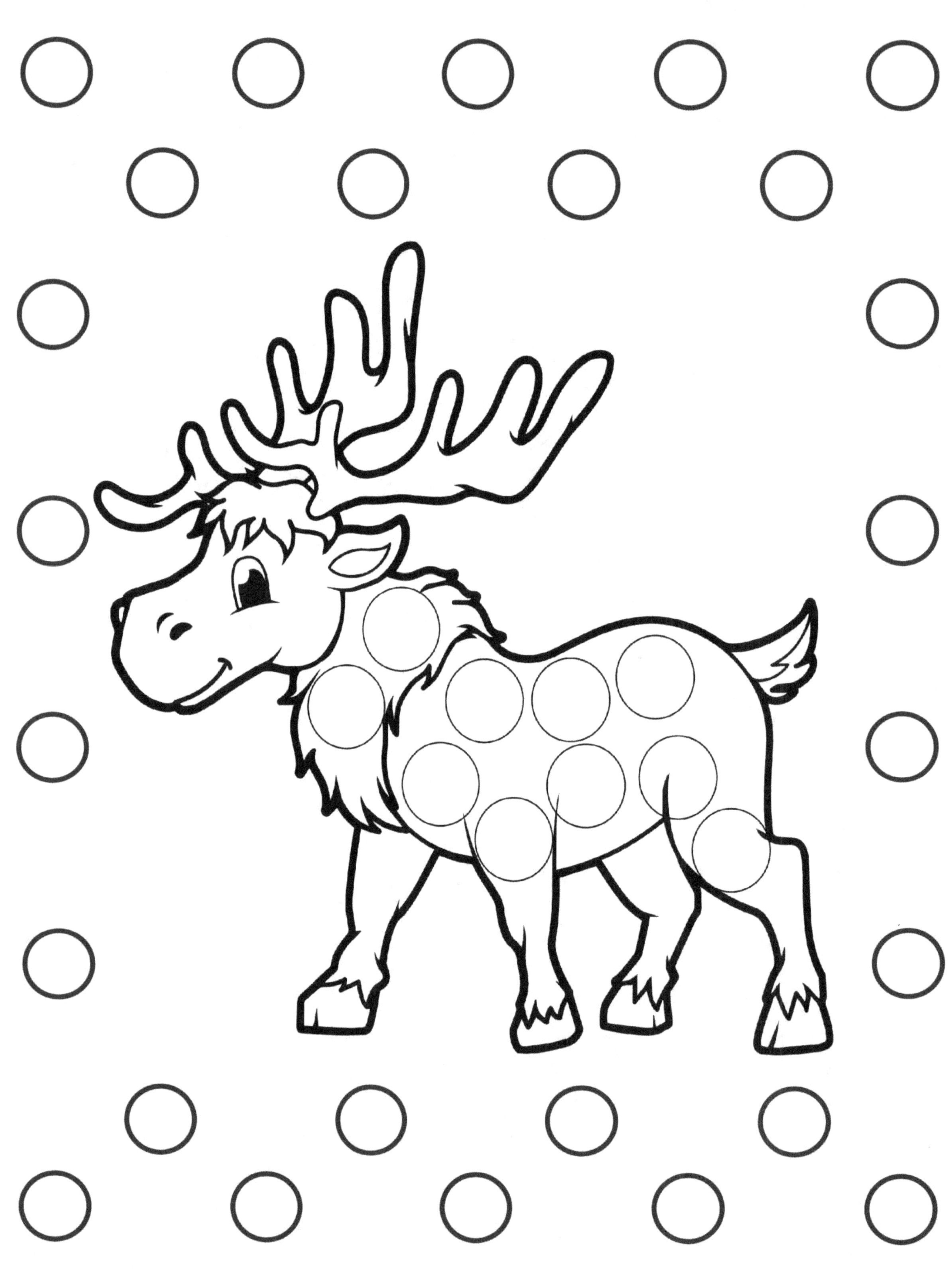

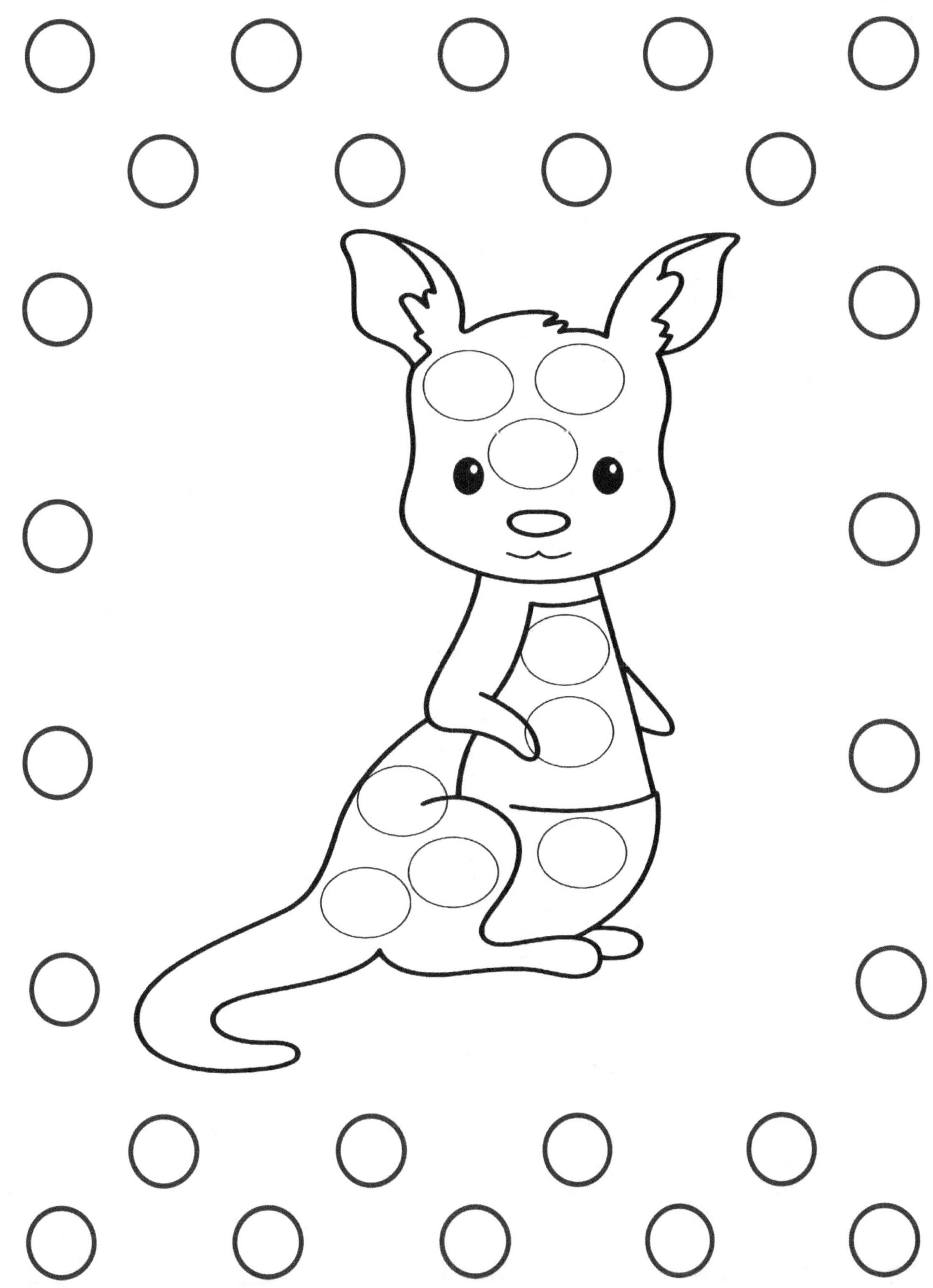

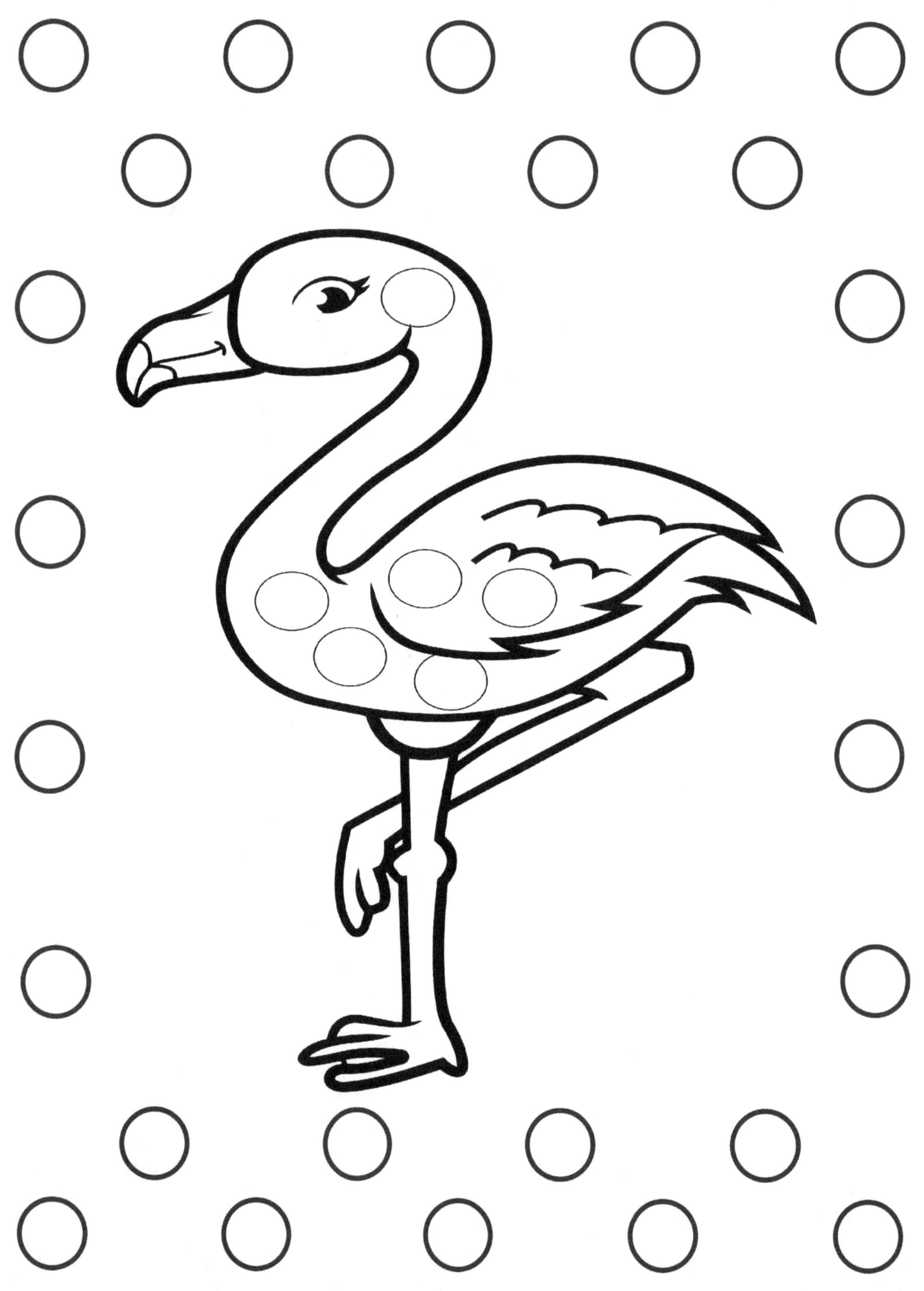

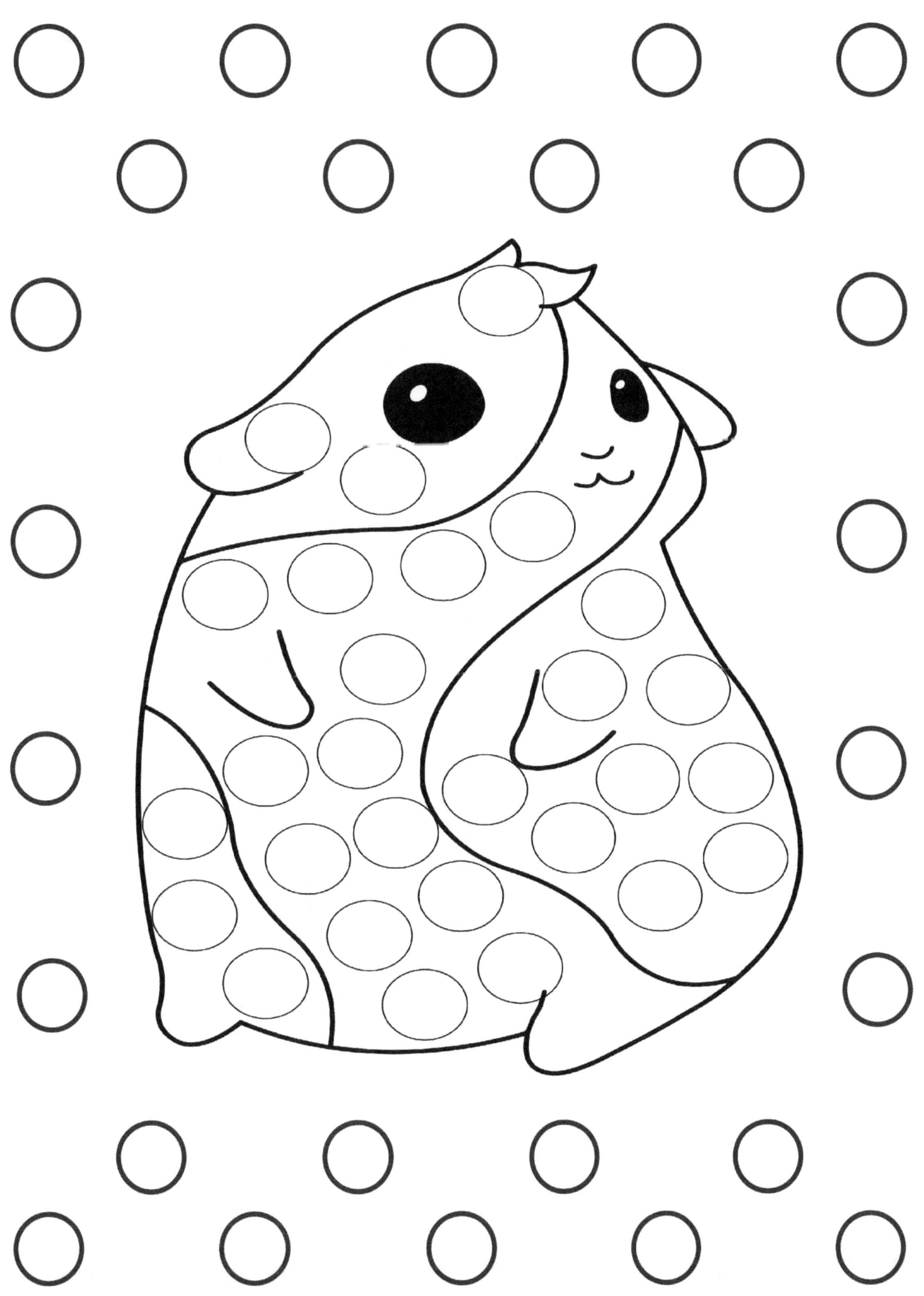